WILD
NIGHTS

WILD NIGHTS

Summersdale Publishers Ltd
46 West Street
Chichester
West Sussex
PO19 1RP
UK

www.summersdale.com

Printed and bound by CPI Group (UK) Ltd, Croydon, CR0 4YY

ISBN: 978-1-84953-699-8

Substantial discounts on bulk quantities of Summersdale books are available to corporations, professional associations and other organisations. For details contact Nicky Douglas by telephone: +44 (0) 1243 756902, fax: +44 (0) 1243 786300 or email: nicky@summersdale.com.

WILD
NIGHTS

CAMPING BRITAIN'S
EXTREMES

PHOEBE SMITH

summersdale

PHOEBE SMITH

Having grown up on the edge of Snowdonia National Park, in North Wales, Phoebe's love of dramatic landscapes has taken her on walking and backpacking adventures all around the world - from wild camping on the Scottish islands, sleeping under a swag in the Australian outback, pitching a tent among penguins in Antarctica and watching the Northern Lights from a wigwam above the Arctic Circle. Phoebe is an award-winning editor of Wanderlust travel magazine (Editor of the Year 2015 PPA New Talent Awards) – but of all the places she's been it's the UK that holds a special place in her heart and she is adamant that you don't need to travel far to have an adventure. Phoebe has written extensively for a range of newspapers and magazines both in the UK and overseas, and is also author of *Extreme Sleeps: Adventures of a Wild Camper*, *Wilderness Weekends: Wild Adventures in Britain's Rugged Corners*, *The Camper's Friend*, *The Joy of Camping*, the *Peddars Way* and *Norfolk Coast Path* guidebook and *Book of the Bothy*. When she's not planning her next escapade she's most likely found in the mountains with her trusty tent or bivvy bag.

For Neil, who's always believed in me no matter what. And for my granny, Margaret Smith, whose tales of her wild adventures during the Second World War and beyond made me grow up knowing that there's nothing a woman can't do.

Finally, this book is dedicated to all those people who have told me that reading about my early wild camping mistakes and escapades has inspired them to get outside – you make every difficult river crossing, every new blister and every worn-out pair of walking boots worthwhile...

Glencoul

Dunnet Head

Grid Ref NH02020 77000

Craig

Ben Nevis

Corrachadh Mòr

N

Scafell Pike

Whitendale
Hanging Stones

Holme Fen

Snowdon

Lowestoft Ness

WILD
NIGHTS

Lizard Point

CONTENTS

FOREWORD

By ALAN HINKES OBE

The only Brit to have climbed all 14 of the world's highest mountains over 8,000m high

Unorthodox Nights, Crazy Nights or Gnarly Nights might come to mind when reading this stimulating book. I blatantly admit to respect for Phoebe tinged with some envy, as this book is about adventure and I like adventure. I have always revelled and taken great delight in exploring the British countryside, as she does.

My mountaineering career started in Yorkshire exploring the local terrain near where I lived and making my own adventures in the woods and becks. When I got into my teens these mini-expeditions and adventures progressed to the hills, mountains and rock faces of the North York Moors, Yorkshire Dales and Lake District, where camping or sleeping in YHA hostels allowed me to explore and expand my adventures.

I have had a few wild nights in the British hills myself, and sometimes just for fun I would sleep out in a basic bivvy bag – a big heavy-gauge polythene sac, big enough to cover a sleeping bag. I even tied myself onto ledges on rock faces as practice for sleeping or bivouacking on big vertical rock walls in the Alps and higher mountain ranges. Some friends understood and even joined me, others could not be enticed, it seemed uncomfortable or dangerous to them – too wild!

I have had some near-death experiences and close shaves on some of my expeditions, especially in the Himalaya, but I do not have a death wish, I have a life wish and adventure enhances my life. Like Phoebe I have had great fun and rewarding experiences in the UK. One memorable mini-expedition I had was to summit all the high points of the 39 English counties in a week. This was a fast-moving, physical challenge, as some of the high points are big hills, and it required intricate route planning and navigating through England.

An adventure does not have to be abroad or death-defying. Phoebe admirably proves this and delightfully describes her experiences here in *Wild Nights: Camping Britain's Extremes*. It does involve a certain level of risk and danger, though, as she is frequently alone on mountaintops, far from the shopping centres, supermarkets, takeaways, TVs, pubs, ambulances and A&E facilities which we all take for granted.

It takes enthusiasm, drive and determination to plan and have a fun adventure and a successful expedition; Phoebe has plenty of these qualities as well as a real sense of humour, which is an essential trait when the going gets tough. She genuinely enjoys her adventures, conveying them graphically with vivid, entertaining descriptions of her escapades.

Phoebe does not have a beard, she is not a hard-core climber, tough mountain guide, wiry fell runner, salty sea-dog sailor or any other specialist full-time adrenaline junkie. She has a full-time job as a successful journalist and travel writer. I first met her in the Lake District when she was a features writer for an outdoor magazine and we have spent several days together in hills.

She has shown skill in planning as well as pluck and resilience heading out alone and map reading, navigating and camping in the wild, remote parts of Britain. Some might term solo camping or sleeping out in extreme places quirky or eccentric – I would prefer to term this behaviour curious and exceptional. I empathise totally and applaud her.

Phoebe has broken boundaries, showing people what can be done in the UK, inspiring and empowering everyone to get into the outdoors and have an adventure. And I hope it inspires you too.

Alan

INTRODUCTION

It all started in Kendal during an argument with a cyclist. Not on the road, you understand – this wasn't a near-collision or a quarrel about rights of way – this was in a pub. There we were sat at the bar, enjoying a particularly rich pint of the locally brewed ale. He had just been telling me about his most recent trip on two wheels following in the tracks of the Tour de France. I was recounting my experience the previous summer pedalling my way through Austria, Germany and Switzerland in a week. Then it happened.

A couple, who were standing at the bar waiting for their drinks, were looking as if they knew me. The woman said something to the man, who then looked down at the purple rucksack that was sat beneath my walking boots and nodded. 'Are you Phoebe?' he asked. 'The one who wrote that book about wild camping? I recognise your black-and-blonde hair.'

I smiled; my two-toned tresses had become something of a trademark since working for a hillwalking magazine some years ago. We briefly talked mountains for a couple of minutes, listing the peaks we'd visited that day, before they walked off back to their table.

'You wrote a book?' asked the cyclist.

'Uh-huh,' I replied.

'What's it called?'

'*Extreme Sleeps.*'

'Extreme what?' He pulled a disapproving face. 'Everything has to be extreme these days – extreme this – extreme that – people don't even know what extreme is anymore,' he ranted.

It wasn't the first time a charge like this had been laid at my door. Ever since I wrote my first book – a tell-all and openly honest journey about how I came to love heading off into remote places and sleeping on my own under canvas – I'd been accused of misuse of the word extreme, from Amazon reviews to trolls on Twitter.

The fact is I never wanted to convince people I was doing something extreme. Wild camping is simply sleeping outside of a campsite, a chance to choose a truly remote spot to pitch your tent, to wake up with the mountains as your headboard and the grass as your mattress. It's legal in most of Scotland and also on Dartmoor in England, but tolerated elsewhere as long as you arrive late, leave early and above all leave no trace of your visit. To those who've been doing it for years it's not necessarily considered that adventurous, but to the uninitiated it can be wildly exciting, and that was something I wanted to share. So I filled the book with some of the most basic mistakes I made when I first started out – from forgetting my camping gas to imagining that an axe murderer lurked outside my tent when I heard a twig snap. It was a tongue-in-cheek title, based on the fact that when I first began wild camping on my own in far-flung corners of the UK, friends, family and even strangers would label my antics as 'crazy', as 'misguided' and, yes, as 'extreme'. In a world where health and safety permeates into every facet of our lives, where we even have to label a bag of peanuts with the phrase 'May contain nuts', the idea that a person – never mind a woman – would choose to head into the risky realms of the wilderness by themselves, with no phone reception, to many people does still seem extreme.

It's all a matter of perspective. A big wall climber would guffaw at tackling an indoor climbing wall, but for someone afraid of heights the idea of getting up it would certainly be extreme. An Olympic swimmer wouldn't think twice about front-crawling for several miles, but a novice would find it too extreme to even contemplate. And now I, after many years of wild camping as a woman on my own, in all weathers, don't ever set out believing it to be extreme – but my non-camping peers do. Extreme is in the eye of the beholder.

I didn't ever want to come off the mountain and brag about my conquering of peaks, I just wanted to let people experience the freedom that I felt by leaving the beaten track and the designated campsites and doing things my own way. I had become sick of walking in groups who seemed to believe that a woman couldn't possibly be any good at navigation, couldn't be equipped with adequate hill skills to make it by herself – despite undertaking many training courses and winter skills tutelage. And so I started to head out alone.

I quickly learned that there was no prejudice in the mountains. The rocks don't care who you are, the weather won't treat you differently whether you're old, young, male, female, fat, thin, rich or poor; nature is the ultimate leveller. Both men and women get scared the first time they sleep in the wilds on their own – and they're lying if they say otherwise. But – like anything – after doing it enough you begin to laugh at the things that once scared you, to smile at the prospect of expeditions that previously filled your heart with nervous anticipation, and to get excited about the thought of pushing yourself further out of your comfort zone.

Over the past few years I've met and become friends with people who have done some truly extreme and inspiring things. From climbing sheer rock faces that others told them no one would ever be able to, to crossing oceans by themselves and walking across entire continents – and I truly respect them for it. But until that night in the pub in Kendal I'd never felt the need to do something like that myself, had never been eager to tackle a definable challenge.

After countering my cyclist's criticism for several minutes, with he labelling me a rambler and I playfully calling him a MAMIL (Middle-Aged Man In Lycra), we stopped the banter and diplomatically changed the subject. I finished my drink and left, bound for the side of a fell and a night in my bivvy bag. He was bound for the nearby B&B for an evening watching Saturday-night TV on a proper mattress.

As I lay within the grass, watching the stars glow above me, I mulled over what he had said. Despite all my assertions I couldn't deny that there was something inside my head that was niggling away at me. Doubt. What if he was right? What did I know about doing a properly epic challenge? What happens after extreme sleeps when the 'extreme' word no longer fits the activity? What next after you've got over your fears of wild camping alone, of going to the wilder places and being self-sufficient? I could have lain there angry or upset, spent the evening worrying about it and torturing myself with endless questions. But rather than moping, I decided I was going to address it.

The more I thought about definable challenges – people who have become the first person or the oldest/youngest to do something – the more I began to realise that we can all become the first person to do something. We can all set a parameter and claim a title by doing something that's the long-est, the hard-est, the deadly-est. And so I decided to set up my own trio of challenges to see what completing a self-set series of definable missions that encompassed my passion of wild camping would do to me as a person. To see if a quest to find 'the ultimate pitch' would be any different from just sleeping in a wild place for fun; to see if holding one of these accolades under my belt would change a single thing.

I made a list. A list of sleepable, wild camping challenges I could 'achieve' in Britain, a list of some 'ests' – be it hardest, longest or whateverest. After just 10 minutes I had a sizeable selection to choose from. I settled on the first challenge almost instantly, for it included places I wanted to head to in the next few months. Challenge One: the Wild Nights Challenge. This would see me seeking out the remotest places in Scotland (arguably the wildest country in Britain) and spending a night in each one.

Challenge Two: the 3 Peaks Sleeps Challenge. For this I would be going for height, attempting to summit and sleep on the highest mountains in each of the three countries of mainland Britain – Wales, England and Scotland.

And what about my third and final challenge? This one needed to be a spectacular finale. A more committing and harder challenge than any of them. I studied the list a little longer, mulling over several ideas in my head, then I had it. I would bed down at each of the extremities of my own great country. I would spend at least six hours sleeping at mainland Britain's highest and lowest points, at its northernmost, southernmost, most easterly and westerly places, and also at its geographical centre – no matter where these points might fall. I could use either a tent or a bivvy bag, whichever I deemed the most fitting for the job, and – here was the crux of it, the thing that made it exceptionally tricky within my hectic schedule – I had to do the sleeps on consecutive nights, one immediately after the other, to make it feel like a properly time-constrained challenge. So what to call it? I debated long and hard, playing with words in my head as though trying on clothes to see what would fit right. Then it came to me and I smiled. Just for that cyclist and all those critics out there, only one name would ever do. I decided to name my challenge number three: the Extreme Sleeps Challenge..

With the gauntlet thrown down and a whole host of new adventures decided upon, I slept soundly that night, knowing that the next few months would become some of my wildest dreams...

ONE:

WILD NIGHTS CHALLENGE

CHAPTER ONE

GLENCOUL

I'd never considered that I might die in Kylesku. When I'd rocked up to the car park in the tiny Sutherland hamlet late on a Saturday afternoon to tackle the first in my trio of remote Scottish outposts in my Wild Nights Challenge, the rain struggling to do any more than release tiny pellets in a lacklustre kind of shower, death was the last thing on my mind. I was instead much more happily distracted by the grey seals popping up with increasing curiosity as I began to make my way along the edge of Loch Gleann Dubh.

Yet it was here, hours later, that I found myself chest deep in river water – the kind so cold that its icy fingers seemed to tighten their grip around my chest, making each breath come out as a small gasp of air. My heart was beating fast with adrenaline, my body fighting to remain upright in the current. The fast-flowing water seemed to echo louder and louder in my ear and though the safety of the bank was less than a metre away from my current point it may as well have been miles. It seemed that here I was, far from civilisation and stuck at a halfway point between living and dying, between the certain hypothermic death of the river and the dry land of survival.

It wasn't supposed to have been this difficult. It was supposed to have been a long but straightforward meander to a once-lived-in estate called Glencoul, where a small uninhabited hut known as a bothy lies in wait for walkers to take refuge in. I had researched it well before I came here, learned all about the Elliot family who, in the late 1800s, had left their lives in the coastal town of Gairloch to relocate into the middle of the mountains, to this lonely cottage on the edge of a loch.

The idea of it had fascinated and enthralled me. Ever since I began wild camping and seeking out the more rugged corners of my island home of Great Britain years ago, I had wondered what it would be like to spend an extended period of time actually living and existing in one of the remote regions of the country.

Through my reading I knew that only the very hardy could and would survive out here, and Margaret Elliot was undoubtedly one of them. She had moved to Glencoul when her husband John got the job of deerstalker in what we now call the Reay Forest Estate. Their home was a fairly large-sized house perched above Loch Glencoul. The only ways in or out were (and still are) by boat, which takes the best part of an hour even with today's engine-powered beasts, or on foot, which takes at least 6 hours of hard graft. Self-sufficiency was clearly key, and Margaret had it in abundance. She raised sheep, pigs and chickens to supply them both with meat and eggs. She also kept cows for milk, from which she made her own cheese, butter and cream. Her husband's job meant that at least venison was often an extra source of food and she would not only cook it to eat the day it was brought to her by John, but would also dry it out and salt it so that the remainder would keep for months – especially important come winter when they would effectively be cut off from the market towns that they relied on for extra supplies.

I thought about Margaret as I paced the pathway that afternoon, encased in the relative warmth of my Gore-Tex layers. I would only be staying for one night, of course, but it was still important that I alone carried everything I would need. In my backpack was a hearty sandwich that I would save for my first stop at the Glendhu Estate – my halfway (ish) point. I also had a handful of hot-drink sachets, a dehydrated camping meal of vegetable curry, a spare canister of gas for my camping stove so I could be sure to boil all the water I needed for cooking and drinking, a porridge for breakfast and a bag full of snacks (cereal bars, chocolate and nuts) to sustain me on my journey. It was a far cry from some of my escapades when I was first finding my feet as a wild camper. Back then I forgot to buy new gas for my camping stove, ran out of food and forgot my suncream. Now I always double-checked my resources as part of my planning, always had plan B routes in case the weather turned, and always kept my well-stocked Go Bag (a bag made up of all my essential kit and some food) in the boot of my car so that there was never an excuse to not have an adventure.

I walked smugly that day, ready for whatever would be thrown at me. Margaret would have been proud.

The path rose and fell alongside the water in an odd chain of twists and turns. For several metres it would be well defined, obvious and clearly ridden by quad bikes or 4x4s, to the extent that it felt at odds with the isolated location. Then, just one turn later, I would be meandering under a thin canopy of trees, the ground a smattering of broken stone. Another turn again and I reached the waterfalls at Maidie Burn, where a small modern hut sits to monitor the water flow and where hydro-electric-generating pipes are laid – it was like being in a factory and any minute I expected some fluorescent-vested men to come traipsing along to tell me to stay away from their workplace.

Not long after I passed a couple, both wrapped up warm against the rain, which was getting increasingly thick. We all nodded to each other, our respective mouths not even visible hidden behind our waterproof chinguards. Another kilometre on I spotted the last of the walkers that day, another couple, their expressions also veiled behind Gore-Tex.

As I passed them I mentally ticked off the cars I'd counted in the car park to work out if I might have a bothy to myself. By this point it seemed that two were still unaccounted for. Before I reached the old Elliot house at Glencoul I would first stop at the other highland estate, Glendhu.

Unlike Glencoul, which I was heading to for its remoteness, Glendhu is still very active. Consisting of about four buildings and reachable by the best (i.e. Land Rover-friendly) part of the track, it's a place where many a shooting party still begins and ends. In the key culling season between August and September you still have to call ahead to make sure it's safe for you to wander here. Luckily for me it was only May.

Not long after the waterfall the path swung back to the very lip of the land above the water. It started off quite low to it, so much so that you could easily dip a toe into the loch and still remain sitting on the path (just about). But then, mere footsteps later, the trail suddenly rose to at least 10 metres above it, the loose stone splinters that covered it falling into the water as I walked on. Now it felt like a proper walkers' path had been reached. Now I felt that the real wilderness beckoned.

The rain began to fall harder, heavier, faster. I knew the dry haven of the bothy couldn't be that far now, but distances are never true on the ground in the misty Scottish 'dreich'. I desperately needed a pick-me-up – a chocolate or sugary sweet, something – but, deciding instead simply to dangle the promise of one in front of myself to spur me onwards, I restrained the urge to stop.

It paid off. Only 15 minutes later (a long 15 minutes, I hasten to add) the narrow gorge-like path emerged lower onto flattened rounded grass. I could see the head of the loch narrowing into the cleaved valley where the bothy lay. I spotted the first, then the second, and then the rest of the buildings appearing a few hundred metres in front of it. Relief.

The grass was saturated with water and squelched noisily under my feet as I neared the building. The unmistakable shape of a boot print, followed by dog paws, shaped the mud, and I readied myself for conversation.

'Hello?' I called as I pushed open the friendly green door and waited to see if my call would be answered.

It was not. And so I busied myself with preparing a hot coffee by the fire, the smell of burning wood past hanging in the air like burnt toast, whisking me back to memories gone by at other such huts deep in the hills.

While the stove sputtered into life and the water began to fizz I nosed around the place. The room where I sat was the main one, complete with a fire grate and benches. Across the entry hall sat a second, with another fire and benches and a table. Both rooms were of ample size. A steep staircase led to an upper level where two rooms, one on either side of the stairs, greeted me. Both had a skylight, making them bright and airy. One even had a small fireplace.

All at once I wanted to abandon my plan for Glencoul, and with it my entire challenge and stay here instead. This was early days in my forays with clearly defined missions and I was struggling with having such rigid boundaries. I mentally picked out my room and in my mind fast-forwarded to the evening, the house warmed by the glow of fire, me snuggled inside my sleeping bag, watching the stars from the skylight overhead.

The sound of water spitting from my cooking pot brought me back to the here and now and I ran downstairs to turn it off. I made my drink and ate my chocolate bar quickly and noisily, with no one there to judge my savage-like eating. My only companion was the skull of a prize buck, complete with huge antlers, a former trophy from one of the estate shoots, sitting across the table from me. In an attempt to avoid its gaze, I found the bothy visitor book and began to read the entries inside:

April 21
Arrived to find the bothy had one occupant already so I took the second upstairs room. We talked a little and I found that he had come over from Glencoul where he said he had enjoyed the place to himself.
Dave, Aberdeen

April 22
A full bothy tonight! Decided to continue on to the car rather than stay. Nice little place though, would have liked to try Glencoul but weather kept me back.
Richard, Edinburgh

April 23
Met a Swedish couple here tonight, who had come over from Glencoul – said they had it to themselves. I may try to venture over there tomorrow if the weather allows it.
Peter, Dartmoor

April 24
Weather bad when I woke up so decided not to venture further. Met a guy from Norway who had set off early from Glencoul. He said it's very wet over there. More people arrived to have their lunch here. Have decided to go back to the car and try further south.
Peter, Dartmoor

And so it went on. Tales of the fabled and idyllically empty and remote Glencoul bothy, with this one every night seemingly occupied. I went further back, to March, then February and even December and still the same pattern emerged. In my mind the hut I had only moments ago seemed set on abandoning suddenly held all the promise of a Shangri-La. I had to get there. The challenge was on.

With a renewed sense of determination I drank the last of my coffee, which had gone cold while I'd been distracted with all my reading. I winced as I swallowed it, the bittersweet conglomeration of coffee granules and sugar congealed into a sludge stinging my tongue. Then I threw everything back into my pack and braced myself for rain.

I wasn't so eager that I didn't take a couple of precautions before I left, though. I know from experience how a few minutes spent planning can make all the difference. I ran back upstairs to the skylight, map in hand, and scanned the rising hillside on the opposite side of the loch. The track there was marked on the map, but whereas the one I'd taken over the last 8 kilometres was marked by the double, parallel, broken lines that signify a proper track, that one was signified only by a single, black dashed line, showing that there was something, but it would be much less obvious. I knew that once I hit the rocks at the confluence of the Abhainn a' Gleann Dubh, finding it wouldn't be so easy. So I counted the water flows I would cross before I found it, looked for large rocks that I could tick off to tell me I was in the right place and spotted clumps of bushes that I'd know would mean I had gone too far and needed to backtrack.

Not for the first time that day I left the safety of a dry space feeling self-assured, impressed by my own foresight. Gone was the klutzy walker and wild camper of the past; I knew what I was doing and strode off self-assuredly into the rain.

Finding the path was easy now I had a plan in place. I kept low to the water line, avoiding the rocks made slick with seaweed and kelp from high tide – which I imagined in the past I might have slid and tripped on with eager anticipation – picked out a giant boulder that denoted the path would start behind it, counted my streams and, before I knew it, began the steady ascent uphill.

With only the walk ahead of me I thought now of Margaret Elliot of Glencoul once more. Not only did she have herself and husband to worry about feeding and clothing, but while living in the folds of the estate she also gave birth to and raised five sons. The first came in 1891 and was named William. Following him came Alistair, Matthew, John and, finally in 1901, James. Caring for a husband and five children, as well as maintaining a house, in such a wild area would have certainly been a challenge, I thought, though perhaps it was a welcome distraction from the fact that she was so far removed from the rest of society. At the bothy itself is a series of printed pages, extracts from the diary of her husband, so an account of their experience of raising a family in such a place has been saved for posterity.

But being able to sit and read about that would not come for me yet, and I was torn from my thoughts by a sudden blast of wind. Lost in my imagination I had almost reached the 205-metre spot height marked on the map, the point where I would turn my back on the Glendhu valley and begin my descent into Glencoul.

Any dreaming of an idyllic life here would have to wait as it took all my effort to stop from falling backwards, such was the power of the wind. I had never experienced such ferocious gusts as the ones I met there – and so low down. The metric height belies the views, though – especially when water is all that surrounds you on both sides. As the wind whipped my hair into a temporary cat-o'-nine-tails, and seemed to suck out my breath as I attempted to pull it back in, I pushed down closer to the ground and almost had to claw my way along in a crouched position. The rain blasted into my face, stinging my eyes like sandpaper. It was hard to see anything.

Over the past few metres the path had become less distinct due to the rain but now it was virtually non-existent. Seeing the loch water below I was desperate to follow a faint deer track downhill, lose height fast and regain the ability to breathe without the battle. But the sensible side of me kicked in once more. I checked the map to realise that my track would at first climb a littler higher and that if I did follow the route down, as I wanted to, I may become stranded on a sheer drop above the water.

Tears streaming down my face from the squall before being pinched away and flying off into the oblivion, holding my hood to my head with one hand, I fought onwards. Every step laboured, every thought focused on the simple task at hand: putting one foot in front of the other, trying not to tumble down the mountainside.

Beinn Aird da Loch is the name of a 530-metre spot height above where the path was cutting alongside the slopes. Looking at it on the map you can see immediately that it's made up of a mass of small tarns, dotted about it like blue blemishes on a teenage face. Seeping off it – particularly to the south where I now was – is a vein-like network of streams, each one making their way into the body of water that is Loch Glencoul below or into the river that feeds it.

I had that image etched into my mind as the path finally began to head downhill. Grassy tussocks helped take out some of the worst gusts before reaching me and I made the first two crossings of water without much more than a stretch of the legs. The rain had turned to a hard hail, making it difficult to look at anything more than my feet but I still felt good about my progress. Soon I was lost to my thoughts once more, imagining the weathers that John Elliot and his sons would encounter on their shopping trips. They usually took their own small vessel over the water to where I had my car parked just over the bridge that was way behind me now. Back then there was no bridge, just a rudimentary passenger ferry to help people cross the water at Garbh Eilean. After that it would be a further 9 miles by road – and that was only one way.

Wondering just for a split second if I should have attempted a watery attack on this place rather than an approach on foot, I spotted the estate buildings below. Perched on some raised ground above the water sat a huge stone house complete with gabled windows and a slate roof. In front of it a smaller building was attached – the bothy. Nearer to the river was a ramshackle barn made of crumbling stones and a corrugated-iron roof. From my heightened viewpoint I could take in the whole estate and – despite the wind and incessant rain – I smiled at the thought of spending time here.

It was not long after this, not many minutes after I had pulled out my camera to try to capture an image of this deliciously remote place, that I realised the path in front of me was missing. I hadn't lost it, you understand, and I hadn't been so wrapped up with my surrounds that I'd strayed off it. No, the path literally dropped away at my feet. It was now that I realised that the two other 'river crossings' that I had naively thought I'd already made, were in actual fact new, unmarked streams created on the side of the mountain by the rain – not actually marked on the map at all. The first of the two main waterways I would have to cross was still ahead and it had been falling with such ferocity that it wasn't only water that it took plunging off the hillside with it – it was the path itself.

I stood transfixed for a second, monitoring the heap of mud and stones that had slipped away and watching the waterfall that it had now created. I could see the bothy, though. There still had to be a way forward.

Slowly and carefully I stepped down off the path, digging my heels into the softened ground purposefully, as if walking on snow. Using my walking pole for stability I continued on a few metres, not moving one foot until the other was firmly in place, and eventually found a narrow enough section to cross. One down, one to go.

The next stream had chopped up the landscape even more dramatically. Exposed deep-chocolate-brown mud had been scooped away as though it were merely ice cream, leaving a gouged-out slice of the hillside through which the waterfall flowed like churned milk. This one was going to need a bit more thought.

I walked up the mountain a few metres to see what it was like but the rocks made it impossible to gain much height. So I tried the other way, heading downhill. Each potential crossing point looked either promising at first but then went too deep and too wide at the finish, or started off potentially tricky and then went easier as it neared the other bank. After deliberating for a few more minutes than perhaps I should have, and getting increasingly soaked from the rain, I went with the latter.

This was going to be like a ghyll scramble I once did in the Lakes. Edging myself off the path I slipped and slid down to a large boulder, just flat enough to support me but round enough to mean I was glad of my walking poles. Faltering on top of it I had to make a leap of faith to another smaller protruding piece of granite. Teetering from that to another, larger offering in a single step I finally reached the mud bank on the other side and attempted to claw my way up onto the grass. It took three attempts but I heaved myself out of there. Not long to go, I thought to myself, again smugly, all obstacles avoided.

I'd been so focused on getting myself over the river that I was surprised when rain began spitting in my face once more. It hadn't relented at all and the bothy below now was merely an imprint against the grey. So I continued, the path taking me down more easily now, the land wet but stable under my boots.

For this particular trip I had ditched my cracked leather footwear for a more nimble lightweight offering, which was meant to be waterproof. In weather like I was experiencing, however, it was not holding the liquid at bay and already I could feel the sting of a blister forming between my toes and on the ball of my foot. It wouldn't matter anyway, just a little further and I would find myself quite alone in this wonderful mountain hinterland, left free to imagine life for the Elliot clan atop a hillock above this lonely loch.

So full of self-assured confidence was I that it took me a while to work out what was wrong with the next sight that greeted me – the Glencoul River. There was nothing odd about the watercourse per se, nothing strange about this fast-flowing water gushing so fast that the whole stream looked more white with froth than blue like it should be. It was just that there was something... well, something missing.

The footbridge. A simple enough invention, a couple of planks of wood spanning the white water, it was clearly marked on the OS map I had in front of me, but it was now gone. Not a single nail or section of wood remained. I pulled out my map again, wanting to check that I hadn't been mistaken, that I hadn't dreamt up the friendly 'FB' symbol when planning the route. I had not; it was clearly there in bold black ink. The footbridge was missing.

Trying to hold back my rising panic I scanned the map for an alternative crossing point upstream. Following it with my finger I went up and up to the point where it folded away in my map case – it was over 5 kilometres away. Still, there was no alternative. If I wanted to reach my paradise accommodation, to complete the first night of my challenge, I was going to have to get across.

Common sense should, of course, have prevailed. But something had happened to me. I was now under the onus of challenge fever – similar to what happens to people in the high mountains with summits. My goal was set; I had to make it.

'Go back to Glendhu,' a sensible voice whispered in my head, 'you have time, you can be back in the upstairs bedroom in safety and warmth in the next 4 hours, just before it goes properly dark.' But I would not listen. Salvation and success was less than 10 minutes in front of me, all wrapped up in the four walls of a waiting bothy.

The rain was getting heavier and the thought of dodging those landslides again, of topping out at that wind tunnel on the 205-metre spot height once more, of carefully climbing down to the bridge and – most importantly – admitting defeat, was simply not an option for me. I was blinkered.

I went first to the loch edge where the river gushes out into it. It looked almost a metre deep, but it was perhaps the widest part – usually the shallowest of any river – and if I were to lose my footing there a fall could mean being shot out into the depths of the loch itself. I headed further upstream. Narrow rapids had formed around the boulders, meaning that though the crossing was short in terms of distance the force of the water would have made it impossible to wade through. I went further up still and found a wide, fairly fast-flowing section that looked no more than about 30 centimetres deep, but the riverbank on the other side had disintegrated, meaning that even if I did make it over, climbing up onto it would have been problematic to say the least.

I continued further up, convinced that the perfect section to cross at would present itself as if by magic. It didn't.

I simply found more of the same problems, one after the other. I kept throwing in rocks to assess the depth, kept trying to calculate which gave me the best odds of success. I headed up so far that I began having to cross subsidiary waterfalls tumbling into this stream. By the time I crossed the third of these my legs were already wet up to my knees.

'ARRGGHUUUU!' I yelled to the air, sick of pacing this final obstacle that stood steadfastly between me and the bothy. Then I got angry.

'That's it, I'm doing it,' I said loudly and marched my way back down to nearer the building. I was intent on choosing one of the options nearer to it, because at least then I would only have a very short walk to make on the other side before I reached my goal and a warm fireside.

My feet now stinging all over in their dampened state, I chose the first section I could find and, without thinking, plunged in. Immediately my boots filled with water, the pressure forcing my trouser legs tight around them so that they seemed to suction themselves to my calves. I thought I was cold when I began, but now my feet were beginning to go numb, such was the chill. I moved slowly using my walking pole to create a tripod of my two legs and it, sidestepping, facing the torrent, remembering to keep two points of contact with the riverbed at all times. Halfway across and it was above my knees, and then about a metre from the bank it happened.

I put my right foot forward and leaned my body weight towards it to help it find ground. Promptly I sank right up to my chest. Immediately I gasped for breath as though I had been winded in my stomach, the chill of the water spreading all over my body. The other leg slipped forward to join it and I felt the weight of my rucksack beginning to pull me down. I tried to move my right foot again, but being pushed down by the current I couldn't do it. I tried again – nothing. Looking up I could see that mud and rocky debris were slowly making their way towards me in the water.

It was only then, in that second, that I suddenly thought about what a dire situation I had landed myself in. Here I was, miles from anywhere and anyone, hell-bent on a self-set challenge, with no one else knowing my plans, trapped in a river in the driving rain. The sound of the water was deafening, drowning out all other sounds. It wouldn't be long before I succumbed to the cold. I never thought this would have been the place where I would die, yet here I was, about as close to it as I had ever come before in my life.

I was starting to get confused. Couldn't understand why, when I attempted to grab the large rock in front of me, I couldn't grip it. It took several seconds for me to realise that I had my walking pole still firmly gripped in my hand so my fingers weren't free to grab the rock. I wasn't even shaking now, just stood there, getting colder, wondering what I could do next. Wondering who might find me here. Thinking about what they might think of me. The playful grey seals from earlier and the warm room in Glendhu suddenly felt a million miles away.

Somewhere among those thoughts something in me snapped. I hadn't spent the last seven years of my life journeying around the UK wild camping, learning lessons the hard way, to end it like this.

'Come on,' I goaded myself, 'get out.'

With all the willpower I could muster I leaned forward once more, released the walking pole from my grip and managed to pull myself onto the rock. There I clung for a few seconds, trying to control my breathing, with mud, branches and debris collecting around me and snagging my hair, pulling me back with the current. Then, with another final tug, I launched upwards, my body heavy from all the waterlogged clothes. Just a little further and I would be out. I tried once but couldn't move, then, after some choice words to myself and one more lunge, everything other than my feet had come out. I lay face down in the bank for what must have been several seconds but felt like several minutes, the grass soft against my cheek, the smell of the earth heavenly in my nostrils.

Like a worm I wiggled further onto it, my legs now clear of the stream. I looked back at the river and simply stared, trying to come to terms with the serious situation I had just put myself in, but perhaps, more importantly, that I had got myself out of. I couldn't help, despite it all, to feel more than a little proud of myself.

Just them my body started shaking – violently – its survival mechanism to warm me up kicking in. I fumbled around with my almost numb fingers, trying to get into my rucksack to retrieve a warm layer. It was only when I saw the spatters of water tipping onto it that I realised it was still raining, hard.

Inside my rucksack, despite my dry bag, everything was wet. I pulled out my fleece and without thinking tugged it over everything I was wearing, my body still vibrating noticeably. Every time I breathed in I could feel my whole chest rattle and shake; it was like I wasn't in control of what it was doing. I knew it was the first sign of hypothermia and my body going into shock.

I needed to warm up and I needed to warm up fast. So, glancing back at the river one last time, I began to head up onto the grass, past the barn and all the way up to the bothy.

I couldn't believe it. Smoke was coming out the chimney, swirling in a winding twirl of black and a darkened shadow of a human shape lingered by the door. Crap! I muttered aloud. After all this I wasn't actually going to be able to even get it to myself. With a sinking feeling I continued on to the door, the figure disappearing inside ahead of me.

On the approach I spotted on the doorstep stacks of 12 packs of beer and cider. I looked to my right and spotted a piece of wheelie luggage – wheelie luggage? How had they got that out here, I asked myself. I could hear several voices. All of them belonging to men. It was a stag party – here to celebrate one of their friend's last night as a single man. My timing, I thought, could not have been worse. Once more I was to be proved wrong.

'Come on in,' shouted one.

'Move out the way, boys,' said another as he got out of the chair nearest their blazing fire.

'Do you have some dry clothes?' said a third.

'Here, have a beer,' piped up another as he handed me a can of Fosters lager.

Over the next couple of hours I was treated better than royalty. From being loaned a pair of dry trousers and socks (I visibly wringed mine out to create actual pools of water on the floor in front of the fire to cries of 'My God') to help with placing my kit strategically around the flames to dry out, they even cleared all their stuff out of the second room so that I had a private place to stay – I saw the best of human kindness that night. Any offer I made to camp instead and leave them to their fun they wouldn't hear of, and in the morning they made me a breakfast of pancakes, blueberries and clotted cream, with a large cup of fresh orange juice on the side. They even managed to blag me a place back to shore in their pre-arranged lift with a fishing boat (which went someway to explaining the wheelie luggage).

It was an oddly fitting end to the first sleep in a challenge that had seen me looking for somewhere very remote, to experience a night in the life of the Elliots who had once called this lonely place home. For here, despite being somewhere physically isolated from the rest of civilisation, I had found a whole group of friendly people. For one night I felt like I had joined a big family.

Emptying my kit I discovered that my down sleeping bag was wet, and consequently the night I spent was very cold, but listening to the fun being had by my bothy-mates in the room next door, and remembering the warmth I had felt in their kindness, I slept well.

Rising the next day, I found the bothy book and the entry in John Elliot's diary that joked about him living in 'the glen at the back of beyond', a Gaelic translation of Glencoul. I learned that the bothy was actually a schoolhouse built by the landowner – the Duke of Westminster – and that a teacher had been brought in to school the children here.

I was reading about the mischief he and his brothers got up to when I spotted a ray of sunlight creeping across the wooden floor. Could it be? Pulling on my still-damp trousers I sneaked outside, while the stag party snored loudly in the room next door. Alone, I was greeted by a fleeting peek of what Glencoul looks like in good weather.

In front of the house is a small grassy hillock of no more than about 20 metres in height. I bounded up it to get a good view of the estate and at the top I found a cross inscribed to two of the brothers – William and Alistair Elliot, the two who sadly died in the First World War aged 25 and 24 respectively. There I sat for half an hour watching the hills reflect in the now still loch, until the storm clouds began to gather either side of the water once more.

I had never felt more alive than I did that morning. I looked down at the river that had given me so much trouble the day before and, surprising myself, I felt a pang of exhilaration shoot through me. When I first started wild camping all those years ago, the actual act of camping on my own in remote places felt extreme, but now, with all the other sleeps under my belt, those early ones didn't feel particularly intrepid. I guess it just reinforced my assertion that extreme really is in the eye of the beholder.

And so it was that something happened to me that day. A cataclysmic shift inside me. From setting out on my challenge with a fairly sceptical and nonchalant mindset, not overly caring whether I would really complete my three missions, I was now suddenly determined to see them through. I wanted to test my limits further and if that meant doing the 'remotest', the 'highest' and the 'extreme' sleeps to do it, then so be it. Because there in Glencoul, yes, I had pushed myself to a limit – and perhaps past it – but I alone had also overcome that situation, had risen to the challenge and survived it – and that felt good. No, not good, incredible.

As I sat there to feel the first drops of the next storm coming in, splashing on my forehead, I realised with a growing glee that it's not until we push ourselves past our perceived limits, till we feel so cold and so tired that we feel we can't go any further, that we discover what we are truly capable of. I had done just that, and now I was addicted once more to the thrill of the find. This wasn't enough, this one dice with a tricky situation. I needed more. It was time to head to the second location of the Wild Nights Challenge to try and push my wild sleeping closer to the edge.

CHAPTER TWO

GRID REFERENCE NH02020 77000

The air rattled like sheet metal. White light exploded in a second, lighting the whole mountainous scene with a temporary spotlight, each jagged spire highlighted, each crumbling pinnacle illuminated. Then, in a flash, it was gone and darkness was once more. I was running. Running so fast I could actually taste my lungs burning, like diluted battery acid rising in my throat, and still I ran some more.

After Glencoul, before heading to the location of the next sleep in my challenge, I needed some good, old-fashioned, home-made stodge to restore my depleted energy levels. Heading south I crossed the boundary into Wester Ross and stopped at a cafe to order a tea and a giant piece of cake. While waiting, the girl behind the counter asked me where I had been.

'Glencoul,' I had replied, 'it's a bothy up in Sutherland.'

I watched her facial expression change. 'Near Kylesku,' I added.

'Oh, I know where it is alright,' she replied, 'middle of nowhere out there…'

Of all the clichés in the English language the one perhaps most overused – particularly when talking about heading to wild and remote places – is 'the middle of nowhere'. As a child I'd heard the expression many times and never questioned it, and even as an adult I had been guilty of throwing it around myself without giving it a second thought. But, coincidentally enough, after my escapade up at Glencoul, my next sleep was to be in the actual Middle of Nowhere™. Yes, it really did exist on the shores of Britain.

Before I had found its exact location, when I was doing my research to pinpoint this mythical place, someone told me they thought the official Middle of Nowhere was the Monadhliath Mountains – something I hoped would not be true. Sandwiched between Scotland's Great Glen to the north and the River Spey to the south, they are a collection of rounded and often-boggy peaks, offering a sense of loneliness perhaps, but no real challenging thrill for a walker, because they lack the pinnacled peaks and rocky crags of the rest of the Highlands.

Another well-meaning soul suggested it was somewhere in the barren heartland of Rannoch Moor – an expanse of quivering marshland, saturated to the point that one wrong step could see you sink in up to your waist. Wild, and perhaps extreme in one sense of the word, but nowhere near as mountainous as I would have liked.

Salvation came from a more reliable source – the Ordnance Survey bods themselves. After a quick enquiry, they laid the matter to rest. It seems this wasn't the first time they had been asked to define its exact location, and they had put 'the middle of nowhere' at grid reference NH02020 77000. Why this most romantic of numbers, you may ask? Well, because it's marked as being the furthest distance from any road on the British mainland – a total of 6.48 miles away from one, to be precise.

As soon as I found out, I couldn't wait – I excitedly punched it into my mapping software and waited for the clusters of contours to emerge. When it finally did load up, it was zoomed in too far to instantly reveal its exact location. I scrolled a little to the right and recognised its geography instantly. It wasn't slap bang in the middle of a deep loch, or perched precariously on a cliff face, it was just on an unassuming piece of land, a mere spot on the flank of a mountain – the mountain of Ruadh Stac Mòr.

If the name sounds unfamiliar, I'll enlighten you. Ruadh Stac Mòr (which is Gaelic for Big Red Stack) lies in the heart of the Fisherfield Forest – a now treeless former royal hunting ground in Wester Ross. On the Ordnance Survey map it's a great collection of swirling orange contours packed in generous number between Loch Maree to the south and Little Loch Broom to the north.

I'd been there a couple of times before. Once on an epic four-day venture, crossing it from bothy to bothy, and then again with my non-hill-loving nurse friend Georgina when I did my south-to-north, wild-camping journey to rediscover the adventure that lay in wait in my own glorious country. Now, it seemed, if I truly wanted to camp in the official Middle of Nowhere on this new challenge, it was time to head back.

It's funny returning to a place you've already been to and where you had such epic adventures. It seems familiar but somehow different, the memories like ghosts from your last visit replaying themselves for you as though on a projector screen, the past merging with the present to create the palimpsest of memories. I remember the first time I crossed Fisherfield what a truly mammoth task it had seemed. I rocked up cocky as you like, thinking it would be a long but straightforward affair. Back then I took all the simple things for granted – mattresses, showers, a simple jacket potato. I headed out bright-eyed and full of excitement. If I remember rightly, there had been a few close calls then as well – a couple of tricky rivers, a lot of blisters, the feeling that perhaps I'd taken on a little more than I could realistically handle navigationally, throwing myself a little too enthusiastically down a vertical scree run. But then, once again, I had stuck at it, got my head down and my hands dirty, and pulled myself out the other side. I will never forget the highs I felt at the end. The first sight of my car waiting for me – ready to give my sore feet a rest. The first taste of a hot buttery jacket potato, its skin crisped to perfection, its middle fluffy and light, waiting for me to lunch on in a small cafe in Gairloch. And then, of course, my first night in a proper bed again, after going three nights in a row on hard wooden platforms and floors within barns and bothies.

After my second, shorter crossing with Georgina, when suddenly I was the one with the 'expert' knowledge, I didn't feel that same sense of thrill. I even took her back to the very same cafe where I had enjoyed my fabled potato and even that failed to stir me back into exhilaration. It seems that, sometimes, a potato is just a potato.

Now I would be heading back for the third time. True, it would be on a new mission as part of a different goal, but I needed to do something different to make this feel like a whole new place.

To do that, I decided to start from Poolewe rather than Kinlochewe, the place from which I'd begun my previous journeys. I stocked up on plenty of supplies before I left and headed out on a late-spring morning to give myself ample time to reach it, instead of feeling I was racing against the clock in my usual way.

I set off from the town and began heading deep into the oft-called 'Last Great Wilderness', enjoying the feeling of a new path beneath my feet.

Earlier in the year, I had found myself in a bothy on the Isle of Skye. Known as 'The Lookout', it's a former coastguard watchpost placed on the edge of the northern tip of the island, near the last splays of land known as the Rubha Hunish, which spill out seemingly haphazardly into the sea. Inside there are the usual bothy trappings – the chairs, the sleeping platforms, the visitor book. This bothy, though, had a unique *pièce de résistance* – a 180-degree panoramic window offering its lucky occupants views out over The Minch and the Isle of Lewis and Harris, which forms a major part of the Outer Hebrides. At night it's a magical place. The lighthouses on any sizable patches of land begin to switch on one by one, and their little blinking eyes twirl in constant spins, reflecting on the waves that crash on the rocks below. Seabirds swoop and soar, terns dive and caw, and every now and again pods of dolphins and even – if you're very fortunate – whales can be seen breaching.

On my stay there I was, unexpectedly, joined by a rather sad-looking Frenchman, dressed in jeans and brogues, cold and bedraggled from the storm that was raging outside, and emotionally wrecked by a recent break-up with a girlfriend who was supposed to be with him on this trip. I welcomed him in and gave him the floor to sleep on while I took the bunk bed in the other room. Giving up the view, and the outside entertainment that comes with it, wasn't easy; so as I left and bid him goodnight, I grabbed one of the few books that sat on the shelf on the old fireplace, to help pass the time before I went to sleep.

I hadn't really looked at what I picked up, just noticed that on the cover was a climber, on a crag somewhere in what looked like the Cairngorms. With nothing else to do I snuggled into my sleeping bag and began reading all about his adventures. His name was Tom Weir and I quickly found out that he was one of the first people to make his living as an outdoor writer. Coincidentally, I soon came to his experience in Fisherfield. He had set out, as I was doing now, into the mountains around Ruadh Stac Mòr with a simple bivvy bag in tow. I too had brought my bivvy, certain that a mountainside would not take a full-on tent. According to his tale, he had headed into the wild, determined to pitch up at the side of Fuar Loch Mor below that very mountaintop. He left his bag and began his ascent just as a storm set in.

In the book he talks of racing down through the clag, desperate to save his camp, but all was in vain. His sleeping bag was gone, lost to the wind, his bivvy was ripped to shreds snagged on rocks, and the weather was getting worse. Determined to survive, he packed up what was left of his gear and headed down the Allt Bruthach an Easain into the valley below where he stumbled across the Carnmore estate, which still sits there to this day. Knocking on the wooden door (back then it was still lived in full time) he asked for help and found a family inside who were willing to assist. From hot drinks to hearty home-cooked food he was well looked after. And there he stayed for several days waiting for the weather to improve so that he could tackle his planned route. It never became favourable and with life and responsibilities calling him home, he had to leave and head back to Poolewe as soon as there was a break in the storm.

The more time I spend in and read about the outdoors, the more the human story intrigues me. I loved spending time by myself, soaking up everything nature laid bare at my tent porch, but, equally, I was growing fonder towards the relationships and bonds that form when we, conversely, remove ourselves from the communities where we actually live on top of each other.

As I approached the first reaches of Fionn Loch a few kilometres from my destination, I was experiencing a wonderful warmth from the glow of the mid-afternoon sun. The wind was out just enough to keep the midges at bay, but not so much that it made walking tricky. I skirted the water's edge imagining what might lie on that spot of ground that I knew to be the most remote – a marker perhaps from a previous, equally curious visitor? A makeshift cairn? A patch of grass made bald by all the people who had touched it before me? I couldn't wait to find out.

Soon I began to spy the causeway at the end of the loch that splits off this body of water from the other, Dubh Loch. Beside me the surface was rippling in the breeze, overhead the sun was still intense and I felt little beads of perspiration forming at the back of my neck.

The wilderness of Fisherfield would always appeal to me. Perhaps it was because I'd been here before, experienced it twice even, and it felt familiar. Or maybe it was because the late, great fellwalker Alfred Wainwright warned people off Fisherfield with the deliciously foreboding and now legendary words: 'Weaklings and novices must expect to perish.' I wish they'd put that on a sign somewhere – I'd love to spy it in the heart of this raw beauty and know that for me it didn't apply.

As I crossed over to the land at Carnmore a snapped shard of deer antler rested on the path. Whether the product of a fight between two stags or merely the spoils from a hunting party en route back to the Letterewe estate on the other side of the mountains of Beinn Lair and Meall Mheinnidh, I didn't know, but I picked it up to feel its smooth surface under my fingertips. Its top was sharp and pointed, its root hard and solid, an impressive specimen to look at. I dropped it in its rightful place – it felt like it belonged here – and continued on my way. I meandered lazily, in no particular rush, feeling like I had hours to enjoy the good weather I had been blessed with.

Despite taking my time I soon found myself at the gate that demarks the Carnmore homestead complete with its barn for walkers and climbers, the goodwill of the family that Tom Weir experienced clearly living on today. On my previous visits I had stayed here, but not this time – I had another goal. Instead I patted the wooden post fondly, the memories here as fresh in my mind as though they were yesterday, and continued up the trail beneath the craggy knoll of Sgurr na Laocainn. It was a pull to the top, but the huge steps and almost flagstone-like paving made it easy work. I topped out at the little collection of water at Lochan Feith Mhic'illean and stopped to pull out my GPS.

The mountaintops looked crystal clear, devoid of even a wisp of cloud. I counted myself very lucky indeed. I looked out over Fuar Loch Mor, Tom Weir's intended camping spot when he first came here. To my right was A' Mhaighdean, said to be the most remote Munro in Scotland; to my left was the scree-coated summit of Ruadh Stac Mòr, home of the fabled most remote spot on mainland Britain. At this point I was around 7 kilometres from any road as the crow flies, but a whole day's walk from civilisation in real terms.

By now it was mid afternoon but this far north it wouldn't be dark for several hours still. So I set about creating a picnic for myself by the side of the water. It was a princely dining room if ever there was one. Water on tap for me to boil, either from the stream or the loch, plenty of food in my bag, high-rising mountains surrounding me every which way I looked; in mountain terms, I had an access-all-areas pass to peak royalty.

The wind began to pick up just a little as I polished off the last of my sandwich squares. At first I thought nothing of it. But then, as I began to wash out my cup, I realised with an impending sense of dread that clouds were beginning to form over the peaks of Beinn Eighe beyond. A storm was definitely brewing somewhere and, if it came, I would be in big trouble, completely exposed to the elements. I knew I might have to retreat – and fast.

I packed away my things quickly and continued on the path, as though heading to the mountain itself. Then, just as the rocky flanks began to rise out from the landscape, a granite tooth protruding from its grassy gum, I veered off the path and followed its base around.

The going was tough; a rough collection of scree and boulders adorned this mountain, meaning I was consistently forced to detour up from or around the route I wanted to take. Other than a few deer tracks I couldn't make out that anyone had been this way before me. It seemed that the Middle of Nowhere was definitely not, as yet, a tourist hot spot.

My boots crunched on, over and around the lower flanks. The more I veered to the east, the more I removed myself from the wind that seemed to be coming from further south, and fast. Before I disappeared around the corner I saw the grey clag just beginning to engulf the summit of A' Mhaighdean and knew it wouldn't be long before it swallowed up Ruadh Stac Mòr too.

Still I continued, descending a little onto the more flattened ground beneath the scree. The earth squelched and gurgled with each step I took, saturated by water that had fallen many days previously. Once at the shoreline of the subsidiary part of Lochan a' Bhragharl I took off my backpack and rifled inside for my GPS. I'd input the grid reference I'd needed before I set off and turned it back on to see the little spot that denoted my position now tantalisingly close to the goal of the Middle of Nowhere. A few more metres and I would officially be there.

Making my way up the north-eastern slopes of the mountain I kept my eyes on the tiny, weatherproof screen and watched with glee as my position aligned with that of the grid reference – all at once I had arrived.

As suspected, all that was there to denote this momentous location was grass, the same grass that I had walked on to get here. There was nothing particularly special about it, but then in a way that made it even more special. If I'd arrived to find a garish sign alerting me to it, with fanfare and markers, I think I'd have been disappointed. No, its very appeal was that it was, quite frankly, an unappealing spot.

I set to work unravelling my bivvy bag, taking pains to secure it on this slanted ground – vastly unsuited for a good night's sleep. As I began to fluff up my sleeping bag and stuff it inside, the first spots of hailstone began to pitter-patter on the arms of my waterproof. The storm was beginning to come in. The kind of weather that can either make or break a mountaineer.

Picking up the pace I located my large dry bag and wrapped my rucksack safely inside. I flung off my boots and placed them inside the black rubbish bag I had brought with me – to stop them filling with water – and then snuggled down into the bivvy.

Sitting out a storm inside what is a glorified body bag is never the best way to spend an early evening. I pushed myself in as far as I could, and listened as the tap-tap sound became louder and more persistent. I told myself that it wouldn't last for long, that it was just a temporary storm and would pass – this was summer, after all.

My fingertips were cold. I sniffed with annoying frequency, irritating even myself. I thought of the many people I'd met who swore by the beauty of a bivvy bag, but I couldn't seem to love mine in the same way. It seemed that whenever I used it the weather decided to prove to me that it wasn't the best sleeping apparatus and I lay awake, cold and more often than not damp, and wished I had my tent.

Peering out I looked across at my surrounds, now slowly being swept up by the mizzle into nothingness. It was going to be a long night.

Somehow I must have dozed off because I awoke with a start, relishing in the temporary confusion often felt when waking up in a strange place. I looked around me to see that, though the rain had stopped, the cloud was lingering, caught on the mountaintops like a thick layer of stubborn dust. I reached down into my sleeping bag pocket and pulled out my phone – it was only a little past 7 p.m. My tummy was starting to grumble.

Reluctantly I reached an arm out of the warmth of my sleeping bag and winced as I felt the cold, wet droplets of freshly fallen rain run off the dry bag that contained my belongings. I searched around for the clip and released it, a tumble of rain rushing down its sides. Feeling around with one hand I located the metallic base of my camping stove.

Before long I had set up my cooker, balancing it precariously on a rock alongside me. The sound it made as it began to warm the cold liquid inside was reassuring and I began to imagine how good some hot food would taste. Across the way I began to make out some shapes. I once read an article on how the human brain always tries to identify a fellow human figure no matter where it finds itself or what the shape in question looks like. I'd experienced this many times before, when I'd been quite alone on a mountain summit or exposed bit of moorland and a pile of rocks had instantly – in my mind at least – morphed into the shape of a man sitting hunched on the floor. Fence posts have become wizened old men lowered in a stooped posture, tree branches have become curious walkers and stone cairns a gaggle of ramblers.

So I looked harder, knowing that on this day, in these conditions, what I was looking at was unlikely to be another human being. My astute theory was correct. It wasn't people lingering on the landscape, but deer. First a doe, large and proud, looking directly at me. Then a smaller one – likely her young – staying close, turning in alarm towards every sound, no matter how small: the lapping of the loch water; the long grass sweeping towards her in the wind; a wild camper fumbling around with a quickly overflowing stove.

I turned it off as fast as I could and began to prepare my meal and drink. I don't know how long I sat and watched the deer, or how long they sat and watched me, but we seemed to be at something of a visual stalemate. I often wonder if deer know they reside in such a perfectly wild place, it they ever get the urge to escape the safety of the herd and find somewhere new, somewhere even more wild than this. I peered over at them still, trying to catch their eyes in the hope that I could somehow glimpse deep into their souls and read their thoughts, but all I got back was a persistent stare.

I was the first to give up, the scent of my food too big a draw to resist. Adding some spices onto the meal that I'd strategically packed in my rucksack, I breathed in the scent of oregano and tucked in, glancing every so often to see if my fellow hill dwellers would be coming any closer to me.

The fog was alternatively thickening and thinning, creating a constant peep show, both revealing and disguising the wildlife. I heard the rustle of a rabbit somewhere close by and searched for it in the gloom, but it never did emerge into view. After tidying my rubbish away I simply sat and waited for sleep to find me and, eventually, it did.

I woke later to find that the sunset had been and gone, leaving behind a sort of half-light around me. At least it's not raining, I thought, and turned over to rest some more.

A flurry of raindrops crackling against my waterproof shell stirred me again. It was too cloudy for me to see any stars in the sky. I looked at my clock, it was a little after 3 a.m. and I was suddenly very thirsty. I checked my Sigg bottle but was out of water. With all the willpower I could muster I unzipped my sleeping bag and immediately felt the cold chill of night-time air spill inside. Pushing my feet into my now-cold boots, I shivered. I needed to make a dash for the loch. I yanked on my insulated jacket and began to descend the hillside, hoping that I would be able to relocate my camp after the deed was done.

The water at the loch was icy against my already cold fingers. I filled my bottle as fast as I could, pushing its mouth under the water halfway to try and will the fluid inside. I looked to the opposite bank, half-expecting to see the deer, but they were long gone.

My bottle half full, I headed uphill and made it back into my bivvy and opened it just as the wind blew a huge litter of raindrops towards me, instantly covering my whole camp. I began to boil the stove again, but the flame struggled to light properly in the wind. As it finally caught the gas and began to boil, I willed the time to pass, but it stubbornly ticked by with no more than monotonous regularity. My excursion to the water's edge had left me feeling cold and, despite the down inside my sleeping bag, I was shivering. The rain continued to fall.

I poured the hot water into my cup and watched as it filled up even more with the now heavy rain. It was nearly impossible to drink it, but I gulped it down as quickly as I could, eager to move my limbs back inside the relative warmth of my sleeping bag. The rain got heavier still.

I shoved everything back inside the dry bag and clipped it together, then zipped up my bivvy and lay inside, willing sleep to come and find me and later release me with the warmth of the sunshine. It was not to be. The rain turned quickly to hail again, whipped up by huge gusts of wind that sporadically funnelled their way down the mountain, seemingly finding their way under my sleeping mat and in between every speck of the fibres that made up my sleeping bag. I pulled my hood up over my head and covered my face with the bivvy. The sound of the raindrops hitting it, coupled with the roar of the wind, was so loud that no other sound seemed to exist. A whole herd of deer could easily have been passing right next to me, and I would have been none the wiser.

I lasted until 4 a.m. By then I was lying wide awake, shivering and shaking in an attempt to keep warm. Suddenly a roaring clap of thunder rumbled overhead, its reverb echoing throughout the valley. I once had a friend who got struck by lightning – not once, but twice, and thereby defying the old saying. He was out in the mountains too; a place where storms come quick and can linger long. As I was fairly high up I was in prime striking distance. I lay there for a couple of minutes willing the dark clouds away, but it was no use.

The sky was suddenly illuminated with the flash of lightning. I began to count between it and the next rolling roar... one thousand, two thousand, three thou... BANG!

Less than 3 miles from me the storm was moving in. I had to get out of there, my location dangerous in this place of high conductors. Suddenly the slopes of Ruadh Stac Mòr , aka the Middle of Nowhere, were not a place to linger.

Almost on cue the sky opened up, sending out a torrent of heavy globules of rain that hammered down all around me. To one side small waterfalls of rainwater were beginning to form, my bivvy fast becoming an island within the cascades. The thought of the warmth and dryness of the barn at Carnmore now had all the appeal of a five-star hotel. I felt like Tom Weir must have.

With the rain getting heavier, the roar of the storm moving ever closer, and my little bed threatening to fast become a water slide, I made a decision. I was not going to put myself in danger like I had crossing that river in Glencoul (arguably the deadliest wild night I had experienced to date). It was time to abandon this sleep and make a dash for safety.

I felt happy that a definite choice had been made, but then came the issue of actually uprooting and relocating myself. Taking a deep breath, I braced myself for the uncomfortable feeling anyone who has ever been rudely hoisted from a sleeping bag too early will sympathise with. I reached over to my dry bag and opened it, spilling out the entire contents on the hill, the lot of it instantly drenched in the many puddles that surrounded me. I pulled myself out of the bivvy and in one smooth movement rolled the whole thing, sleeping bag and all, into a ball of fabric and shoved it inside. The rest of my collection got shoved on top – I would sort it out much later. Finally I pulled on my boots, my overtrousers and my waterproof jacket, and then checked the spot for anything left behind. It was all clear.

Time to make a run for it. Leaving my official Middle of Nowhere spot to head just west of it, I made a route for the estate I had passed on the way in. The steps en route were all forming mini waterfalls within mini waterfalls. I tried to use my head torch to see the way but with so much water falling I could barely see in front of my hands, never mind down the hill to the bothy.

Every now and again the whole scene would flare into a dramatic strobe-like clarity, whenever a flash of lightning illuminated the sky. My soundtrack was the growl of the thunder that seemed to regurgitate again and again deep in the mountain's belly. Once or twice the power and strength of the storm stopped me dead in my tracks – I was afraid to move in case it found me.

By the time I reached Carnmore about an hour later, it was already beginning to get light. Head to toe I was dripping with water – as if I had once again undergone my epic river crossing in Glencoul. One by one I peeled off the layers and hung them out to dry on the walls. As I tucked myself inside the womb-like warmth of the barn, sheltered from midges and rain, listening to the wind whistle under the corrugated-iron roof that shook and moved as the storm raged on outside, I wondered if anyone else had come out all this way just to experience that little patch of ground that I had just left behind, that man-defined, certified patch of extreme wildness, just because it was officially the most remote patch of ground on mainland Britain. Considering there's not any real highlight – no mountain summit, no special cave, no really interesting geological patch – I doubted it. But once I publicly revealed it to be so, would someone then come?

I shivered as I thought about my close call with the storm outside. Another dicey sleep in this wild challenge, and I started to wonder if it really was worth the risk. But then, once again, despite the hazardous storm, I had risen to the challenge and pulled myself out of it. Self-sufficiency had again been proven, and I felt greedy with self-pride. And yet, at the same time, something else had happened. I'd been alone, away from other humans, yet seemingly surrounded by wildlife. I'd wanted to experience nothing but the environment around me during this remote-wilderness-themed mission, yet when I truly did, in the form of a violent storm, it was the man-made that I turned to for salvation in the form of the bothy, just as Tom Weir had done before me in this same place. By wilfully disconnecting myself from others I seemed to have somehow become even more connected with them than ever before.

Lying there, the scent of the candle wax filling my nose, I thought more about the idea of somewhere being labelled 'most remote place', and how that designation had been the only reason I paid it any attention. I wondered – could a place ever really be 'the remotest'? Just because you're far away in distance, does that really make you all that far from the rest of the human race? Many people are surrounded by family and friends all the time, yet feel desperately alone. Right now, surrounded by the stone walls that someone had so kindly left available to me, staring into the eyes of the skull of the Highland cow that hung on the wall, I felt very much part of a very special human interaction. And in my next extreme sleep, the final one in this Wild Nights trio, I would feel it once more, only even more intensely.

CHAPTER THREE

CRAIG

From the Middle of Nowhere I headed south to find Craig. Not a man, you understand, but a remote building; a bothy, in fact. But this was no ordinary bothy. Though it now sits under the care and watchful eye of the wonderful volunteers of the Mountain Bothies Association, it was – until 2003 – holder of the accolade of 'most remote hostel in the UK', having at that time belonged to the Scottish Youth Hostel Association (SYHA). Much like the designation of Middle of Nowhere bestowed upon Ruadh Stac Mòr had attracted me, this purposeful singling out of a man-made place as the 'most remote' in a time gone by became the reason I had to visit it. I wanted to see what difference it made to a place to hold an official title like that, to see what happened when the remote and the man-made collided.

Back when it became a hostel, in 1935, visitors would arrive wide-eyed and excited, carrying their luggage on their backs, hopeful that the warden inside would welcome them in to one of the few bedrooms, where a mattress waited for the night. There were hostels all over the UK, of course, but what made this one particularly special was that there simply was no 'easy way' to get there. If you wanted to experience a place as beautiful as this, then – quite simply – you had to put in the effort. With no road to bring in visitors or supplies, self-sufficiency was key. And getting to the end of the road to even start the required trek was (and still is) a mission in itself. Located along the shores of the mighty Loch Torridon in Wester Ross, on the north-western edges of Scotland, the tarmac comes to an abrupt halt next to a cottage in the hamlet of Lower Diabaig, and that stretch of tarmac is itself a winding, narrow road from the nearest town of Torridon a good 30-minute drive away. Here the land juts out into a hulk of headland where no village, convenience store or paved track sits until, 8 kilometres later, by foot, you reach the small fishing village of Red Point. Set beside a pink-tinged sandy beach, this is another hamlet where facilities are sparse and only a single-track road connects it to more lively villages.

Even when it was open as a hostel there was no help for those with too big a load, no respite for the weary. This was a hostel which everyone walked to themselves and where they mucked in to help with the chores when they did get there – whether it was collecting eggs from the chickens for everyone's breakfast the next morning or tending the vegetable patch to create garnish for dinner. The unofficial motto was 'help each other out'. Despite it's closure as a hostel 12 years earlier, I was eager to experience a night in it – with or without a warden – and complete my first challenge in the relative comfort of four solid walls.

I pointed my car first towards Torridon, where the road weaves along the base of sheer rock faces. Though it was way past 6 p.m., nightfall was many hours away. Tents sat below the crags in the free campsite, their roofs still sagging under the weight of the previous night's rainfall. I drove on. On this single-track road people drive along seemingly bewitched by the magic of the mountain scenery and I was no exception. Only the occasional local whizzed by me when I stopped for the umpteenth time to admire my surrounds. But it didn't end there. After the coast the tarmac bends around to veer steeply uphill. Soon Loch Torridon, which only seconds before was a metre below the steering wheel, was hundreds of metres below me. Turn-offs for one-house hamlets began to beckon, rocks cut through grassy fields, views opened out, and the former volcanic past of this region presented itself, the land looking as though it was oozing lava into the cliffs and seawater below.

Finally, after a cattle grid, another sharp right turn saw me in Diabaig. I turned to head uphill until I could go no further. In front of me was a small white house and the road ended. It was time to continue on foot.

Craig was originally built in the 1800s to house crofters and fishermen. It would shelter families who worked the land or sea in this isolated area – even now it's nearly quicker to walk from the settlement at Diabaig to the old fishing hamlet of Red Point than it is to drive it. In fact, unless you have two cars or are rich enough to pay for a taxi, walking is pretty much the only option if you want to efficiently get from one place to another. As there became less need for buildings like this on remote headlands, Craig had begun to fall into disrepair until the hostelling community decided to take it on.

As I got out of the car a white-tailed sea eagle soared overhead and I was hit with the instant briny scent of being close to the coast. I looked around for signs of life in any of the houses, but saw nothing and heard no one. I was quite alone.

Going through the gate I thought of those who came to stay here back when it was a hostel. It must have been quite an exciting and novel prospect back in the late 1930s when it first opened – in fact, back then, just getting to this gate and stepping onto the open tussocks of mahair, the native shell-based grassland, without the benefit of fast, power-steered cars, would have been quite an adventure in itself.

With a jolt the gate slammed shut behind me and I began to crunch my way along the terrain. Though it wasn't yet raining, a damp sense of impending showers lingered in the atmosphere, as though at any minute it would open up and I would be flooded off the rough path down into the sea.

Looking in the mud I saw the unmistakable prints of mountain-bike tyres and wondered whether or not I would have the old hostel to myself. A little further up the track there were paw prints from a large dog, its owner's size-12-boot imprinted steps alongside.

I crossed several small streams as I went – luckily they demanded only a simple leap or minor detour either up or down the path to be surmounted. I had a sudden flashback to hikers in the late 1930s and 1940s traipsing through the mud in layers of heavy clothing, and long skirts in the case of the women, and felt glad to be wearing my water-resistant trousers and Gore-Tex lined walking boots.

Sixty-eight years is an impressive amount of time for a hostel to remain operational – especially a remote one like Craig. I had been sad to learn that the national hostelling network no longer saw it as a viable option, and wondered whether it was just a case of not enough people knowing about it, not caring for its 'most remote' label as I did. If they had known about it, would they then have wanted to save it for the generations to come?

As my way forward became higher above the sea, the panorama in front of me began to really open out. From the promontory before I made it to Lochan Dubh I could spy the little pieces of the coastline that had broken off from the mainland to form their own rocky islands – from Sgair Dughaill in the south to Sgair na Trian further beyond. Ahead I could see out over to the Isle of Skye, where I had met the sad French walker many months ago. Beyond that were the wonderfully long spits of land that make up the Outer Hebrides. Despite a brewing mess of storm clouds, it was still a phenomenal sight.

A shrill wind pierced loudly in my ears as I neared the lochan. The frozen blast of a water-cooled breeze penetrated every weak spot in my hi-tech clothing. I shuddered despite my warm layers.

As I reached the top of the pathway before it descended down towards the bothy, I spotted the mini copse of trees that surround the building. Made up of birch and pine, it had obviously been planted to work as a kind of natural windbreak, designed to protect the building from the elements. From this position my brain once again deceived me as it tried to create a man out of the luminous orange buoy that dangled from one of the tree branches. So convinced was I that this was a walker stood outside admiring the view that I even waved a hello; it wasn't until I descended nearer to it that I realised my mistake.

The rocks were slippery underfoot as I climbed down towards the pathway. I spotted the buoy along with the old fence posts that had clearly been erected a long time ago to try and keep the local red deer out of what would have been a very varied vegetable garden. Now the posts remained, but the fence had gone. Outside the building an old push-along plough sat rusting amongst the grass. Oddly, the lawn behind it was short, whereas in front of it the grass was long, as though the user had just up and left mid job and would come out and continue his chores any second. On the ground in front of me a hand-carved wooden sign lay in the grass. On it in blue paint, inscribed in friendly, large rounded letters, it simply stated Red Point.

I picked it up and pointed it in the right direction, then used a rock to wedge it in place. Then I surveyed my scene. In front was Craig, the stone building with two upstairs windows and two downstairs ones. Above the door swirled a Celtic knot in blue and yellow, the name of the bothy penned within it. To the left I could hear the gush of the Craig River, which was spanned by a metal bridge. To my right the old patch of woodland swayed and creaked in the breeze. Directly in front of the bothy was a path that led down to the sea.

Before exploring that path, I headed inside. Much like the scene of the plough in the garden, as I stepped into the hallway I instantly felt as though I was treading into an old photograph, a time capsule persevering as a moment in time from the past.

Once again I called out 'Hello' when I rapped on the door – once again it lingered there unanswered. I was alone. To the left I entered the main living room, what would have been the hub of activity back during the hostel's active days. The centrepiece of the room was a massive cast-iron stove – one that I later found would not only heat this room efficiently but also the room above it. Perhaps more impressive, though, was the mural. Painstakingly drawn and painted on the whitewashed stone, it was a network of loops and crosses that made up a giant Celtic knot, again in blue and yellow – a larger version of the detail seen above the door outside. Off to the right of this room, behind an old patterned curtain, was a kitchen. I went inside to see the metal-covered worktops, drawers and cupboards, again looking like the chef had only recently left.

Going back into the hallway I opened the door on the other side of the corridor. On it was a sign saying 'Danger, do not enter', so I had to take a look. Inside, some of the floorboards had been lifted up – they were clearly warped and rotten and in dire need of replacement. The room smelled musty and damp and I was quick to shut the door once more.

Slowly, I climbed the stairs up to the landing. There were three doors – all closed. The one on my left opened to reveal a large room – obviously a former dorm, which would easily have taken ten bunk beds, sleeping 20 people. Now, however, it just sat empty and the only thing I could see in there were some discarded sweet wrappers, left by previous occupants. Without hesitation I scooped them up in my hand; I would carry them out the next day.

The second door led to a tiny box room. Featuring two bed frames wedged into position, the light came from a small skylight, which, though modest in size, allowed a huge amount of light. I imagined this space would be a reserved private room for a couple as, even when the door was closed, there was barely enough room inside for two people to stand up side by side – certainly not without stooping over.

The final door intrigued me the most. On it was inscribed 'Warden's Room', clearly a relic from its days as hostel. Above it someone – clearly amused with themselves – had scratched in the words 'Jury and executioner'. I swung it open, expecting to be greeted by someone inside, but there was no one there. It did feel very much like it was well lived in, though. Two metal bed frames filled the floor space. A bookcase filled with tomes lined the far wall and an old metal trunk sat in one corner – the abandoned luggage of the former resident perhaps? On the windowsill were two candlestick holders and beside them a box of matches that revealed itself to be empty.

I was instantly enamoured with the room. I could picture myself living here for the summer season, tending guests and keeping house, carefree in the beautiful folds of the Torridon hills. I set to work organising my gear in case anyone else should turn up. I painstakingly laid my sleeping bag and pillow on the bed frame – which even boasted its own mattress still – and dug out my own tea lights, which I placed in the window frame. Outside the storm clouds lingered out to sea and a swarm of midges gathered on the pane.

Back downstairs I looked on the noticeboard in the main room. There were maps, both real and hand-drawn. One, an OS offering, simply highlighted the route from here to Red Point, a popular there-and-back meander that is something of a right of passage for backpackers in this neck of the woods. Another had been hand-drawn by someone who had had time to spare of an evening. It not only located this bothy and the best place to grab water from the nearby stream, but also kindly noted the worst of the midge fly zones, the point at which ferns reached above an average-sized person's waist. It also noted how individuals, if venturing that far in search of a stone circle marked on the map (which it also helpfully commented was not actually there) would need to undertake a rigorous and thorough body check for ticks once they got back.

Also on the board was an advert for one of the local businesses in Lower Diabaig that sold coffee, tea and cakes to walkers who were making the hike back to civilisation, as well as offering boat tours along the water. After scrutinising the bothy code of conduct and having a second squiz at the map, I set about finding my favourite item – the bothy book.

To my delight it went back as far as 2012 and I began to read with pleasure. Among the thanks and praise for the work done by the MBA in looking after the place, and people telling of ghost stories they had shared around the fire, there were entries left by some who had intimate connections with the place. I love looking at the writing in bothy books – I think the handwriting alone can tell you much about a person, almost as much as the words themselves.

Take Alistair Dickson, who came to Craig during May of 2012. His friendly and open blue-felt-tip print tells of 'the vicious midges' and how his first visit here had been in 1969, when his chore was to help carry up coal that had been delivered for them on the beach.

Then came the curly scribe of 13-year-old Morven later in the spring. She had arrived with her dad, who had once 'a very long time ago' been a former warden for the hostel. She comments wisely: 'It was my birthday and a very good idea to get a teenager away from Wi-Fi and signal for three days!' She also wrote of something that intrigued me – something I'd seen on the hand-drawn map on the wall – a thinking stone.

'Basically,' she explains, 'it's the huge flat stone that you can see sitting here and it's quite high to jump from.'

Next was an entry from John and Vera in July 2013. Penned in scratched joined-up black biro, they write: 'Walked in from Diabaig in the morning. Lovely sunny day. My mother used to look after the hostel in the 1930s. Her family lived in one of the houses down by the water, the one that had the tin roof.'

Reading through those pages gave me as much local knowledge and tips as if the warden was still staying here with me. Pulling on an extra jacket I headed outside to go down to the beach to see the old houses. Before I'd headed to Torridon a quick search had revealed that a small group of native, feral goats inhabited these parts and it was their hotchpotch of a trail I followed now, down amongst the rocks, trees and bushes, to take me to the pebble-strewn beach that lay at the end.

My feet kept sinking far into the mossy ground and, as I was wearing my super-lightweight footwear, my socks were almost instantly drenched. But with the promise of a hot fire on which to warm them on my return, I didn't let it stop my exploration.

Just above the beach proper were the remaining four walls of a shelter, themselves crumbling with the constant battering of sea squalls and salt water. On the pebbles was a host of washed-up kelp and an impressive slice of a tree trunk that someone had crafted into a makeshift bench. I sat on it to watch the sea.

Movement. Something fairly large was walking on the slopes opposite me. I paused, not daring to breathe or move. I was expecting to see a small goat munching through the grass. Instead, however, was the spotty hide of a deer. It was looking right at me, and I at it. There we held each other's gaze, neither one of us daring to be the first to move and break the spell.

This time it was she who relented, turning her head to continue grazing at the grass. Every few mouthfuls she would repeat the process, chewing, looking at me, holding my gaze, then going back to her meal once more. In front of her were two other abandoned houses, though neither was in as good shape as Craig, not being afforded the luxury of guardianship by the MBA. Closer to the destructive nature of the ocean, all that remained were pieces of a rusty roof and tumbledown walls and broken chimneys – certainly not shelters you'd want to attempt a night out in. If it were a choice between them and this beach – I would have chosen the beach every time.

A sudden gust caught my attention and I watched the looming cloud slowly creep inland from sea. The air held the tension of an electric storm. Each minute ticked by and I waited for the rain, but it never came.

Old tyres, buoys and other fishing spoils littered the beach, all looking oddly out of place in this perfectly wild scene. The deer on the hillside was joined by a companion. They both took their time to head towards the dilapidated homesteads – nature reusing our human spoils for their own uses.

I left them to it and, after watching the orange strip of sunlight fade to a darker shade or peach, headed back up the path towards Craig. Almost by mistake I came across Morven's Thinking Stone. A beautifully rounded out slipper-shaped piece of rock that seemed weathered into the mould of a lazy-boy recliner. I fought my way onto the top of it. She was right; it was high to jump off.

There I sat for a while, waiting for the rain to come and force me inside. The odd midge circled me lazily and I was feeling too lethargic to bother to fight it off. I rested and felt my eyelids become heavy. At first I tried to resist. As they battled to close shut, I forced them back open. Soon, however, I lost the will to stop them and in the coolness of a springtime evening I let sleep find me – certain that rain would wake me from my dreams...

CRACK! The snapping of a twig jolted me awake. Immediately my eyes shot open, darting around the surrounds without the need to even move my head. CRACK! There it was again, someone was approaching me from the direction of the beach. Without moving my body I slowly slid my hand into my jacket pocket, my back aching as it pressed firmly against the cold temperature of the rock. Discreetly I pulled my phone up to my chest and pushed the button on the centre – it was nearly 10 p.m. I'd been resting here for a little over an hour.

CRUNCH! Whatever it was, it was coming closer, so now was my chance to get a better look. In the past, when I first became a wild-camping aficionado, any noise like that would have sent alarm bells off in my head. I would have been sure that a mad murderer was coming my way and was out to get me. Experience has, of course, taught me that this is rarely the case. It is nine times out of ten merely a rabbit. The other one time? Just a sheep. Preparing myself for either one of these eventualities I pulled my legs up and swivelled in my seat. It was not what I expected.

Neither rabbit nor sheep greeted me – instead, the devilish eyes of three wild goats, a mother and two kids, looked up expectantly at me. In my surprise I didn't think to get a picture and yelped out a squeal of delight. That I had witnessed these feral creatures without having to seek them out was a real privilege. I watched as the mother led her kids around the Thinking Stone and over towards the river. I climbed up into a standing position so that I could get a better view of them – then the mother disappeared into the undergrowth, heading back down towards the coastline. The first kid leapt down to join her. The second one glanced back to me, let out a cheering bleat, not at all fazed by this odd human, and then was gone too. I smiled.

Gathering my things together I headed back inside to the warmth of the bothy. Even without the fire on it was instantly hotter than the temperature outside. I built up the fire with the wood I had carried in and watched, mesmerised, as it began to light, the flames licking the bark as a dog laps up a bowl of water.

I went into the kitchen to fire up my stove – figuring that I may as well use the room as per its intended original purpose.

I walked over to the window and noticed, with increasing amusement, that there was an outside toilet – one that you flushed using water gathered from the stream. This place really was full of surprises. Looking outside, darkness was still not complete. I picked up the bothy book again to read while I ate.

One entry in particular caught my eye. It talked of an old shelter stone, a place which Neolithic man would have used to sleep in many years ago. By this account it wasn't far from here – merely a kilometre at most. I peered out the window. The storm was still out at sea; its falling rain appeared like a curtain of chain mail against the rest of the sky. It was time for a little expedition.

Grabbing my waterproof jacket, head torch and map I left the comfort of Craig once more. Crossing the bridge, the sound of the river was a constant; the water level had been steadily rising all day. I followed the path down towards the sea and then turned right onto it as though heading to the settlement of Red Point.

Not long after I came to a small stream. As per the instructions I had found, I looked uphill to see the faint indentations of a lesser-used path ascending alongside it. I followed it up on the eastern bank, the wet grass sticking to my trouser legs. I was aiming for a small escarpment of crags. Fallen rocks began to crowd my pathway and I strained my eyes in the dim light, trying to find my way uphill. Soon I noticed what I had been aiming for; a large block of stone coated in a film of heather.

According to my bothy guide, this was the Neolithic rock shelter, which would have been home for man for thousands of years. In front of it was a knot of stinging nettles bursting through the little grassy mound. This, the bothy book had informed me, was a shell midden, which is a layer of earth built up from the many discarded shells left by former residents. It felt unreal to be here, to still be able to see a marker of this place's past use, to hold a connection with my human ancestors who slept wild in a place such as this, not through choice but through necessity.

There I sat for several minutes, imagining them feasting on their shellfish, until I realised it was too dark to see any further ahead than my own hand, my pale skin pallid and almost luminescent in the night.

Carefully I began to pick my way back down to the pathway, heading back to the bothy, my own generation's legacy to the wild-sleeping world. As I found my way over the boulders and overgrown shrubbery en route to Craig bridge, I wondered if, in the years that followed, a curious future soul would come, as I just had, late at night, to try to discover the ruin of Craig once nature had reclaimed it too. Whether they would scan the Thinking Stone for remnants of my evening snack, or try to garner impressions of family group size by the foundations that remained of the other houses on the beach. That thought made me smile a lot.

Back inside the embers of my fire still glowed behind the stove door. Stoking them, I tossed on a couple more pieces of tinder and made myself a hot drink, while watching the curious rain cloud that never was.

Soon I retired upstairs to the luxury of a proper bed frame and mattress. The candle I had placed in a holder and rested on top of the old trunk flickered and spat in the darkness. The bookshelf was cast in a pool of amber glow, and I picked a book up nonchalantly and leafed through its pages.

****

Without doubt this short challenge had encompassed a trio of extremely satisfying remote sleeps. In doing them I had learnt that I had the ability to face some fairly scary situations and get myself out of them. I had felt the satisfaction of completing something I'd set out to do. It had all the elements I looked for in an adventure – some history, a sense of purpose, wildlife, a connection with people from a time gone by, a mission set and a conclusion gained. And, I couldn't help but admit it as I lay there so warm that I didn't even need to tuck my arms into my sleeping bag, I was already looking forward to my next one.

After my dicey river crossing in Glencoul and my run down from the thunderstorm in Fisherfield, it seemed that I needed something risky to make a night out have the desired excitement factor. Climbing the highest peak in England, Scotland and Wales and sleeping atop each of them was certainly going to offer a new set of problems, but also an even bigger sense of satisfaction when I'd finished. I turned over and nuzzled down deeper into my sleeping bag, the down-filled baffles enveloping me in their embrace.

I allowed myself to enjoy this comfortable sleep, knowing that soon, in my next challenge, I would be pushing the boundaries further than I ever had before.

TWO:

THREE PEAKS
SLEEPS CHALLENGE

CHAPTER FOUR

SNOWDON

Snow. So complete and all-encompassing that I could smell it. A damp, chilled inhalation of air stinging at my windpipe with every passing breath. I stopped for a minute, plunging my ice axe into the knee-deep snow, and allowed myself to flop back into it, a makeshift icy chair. Surveying the scene, I could feel my cheeks flushed red with exertion and frozen with the wind chill. Below me the lake of Glaslyn twinkled, its surface edged by a paper-thin coating of frost.

I had decided on something of a whim that this was the night I was going to sleep on Snowdon and begin my 3 Peaks Sleeps Challenge. I had been back in North Wales visiting family, and had spent several days in the comfort and confines of a centrally heated house, complete with memory-foam mattresses and bad TV on tap. It was April, around Easter time, and I had been desperate for some fresh air. So, as with my previous tent-bound adventures that had started several years ago with my first solo wild camp in Snowdonia National Park, I picked up my winterised Go Bag, complete with four-season tent and expedition sleeping bag, and headed the car decidedly towards Snowdon.

I had seen that there would be snow on the summit from the Mountain Weather Forecast before I left, so I had brought some crampons and an ice axe with me so that I wouldn't have an excuse to bottle out of my plans. With its English translation of 'snow hill', it seemed as apt a time as any to aim for a summit sleep. At 1,085 metres high, Snowdon is the highest mountain not just in Wales; it is also higher than any in England. It even reaches way above many mountains in Scotland, at least it does outside of the Scottish Highlands. Its loftiness guarantees it some impressive views, with clear days often boasting a panorama that can include the southern reaches of Scotland as well as parts of England and Ireland, and the Isle of Man. I wasn't going to see any of them that day, I knew for sure – but I also knew, then, that if the temperature dropped, as it was expected to do, a camp at the top would see me receiving the brunt of this deep freeze, meaning a cold night and definitely a crowd-free one.

But I had not expected that I would see as much snow as I had when pulling up at the car park earlier that afternoon at Pen-y-Pass, the highest start point from which people can ascend the mountain. It was difficult even to know that I'd parked in a proper and designated spot, because there was already so much of the white stuff on the ground, concealing the lines under its coating.

The place was filled with the kind of peaceful silence that only snow cover can give. Every sound is muffled – even human voices carry across its surface as only a whisper. With a dirty grey slush of snow appearing around the door of the toilets and visitor centre, and more of it forecast to fall later that evening, I had been surprised to see the number of vehicles in the car park, the owners of which were apparently out on the slopes too.

I left by passing through the gate to the Pyg Track, one that is fairly popular in summer, coming in second, perhaps, only to the Llanberis Path that starts further down in the town. Debate still rages on as to why it is called the Pyg Track, with some believing it has something to do with it passing over a high pass called Bwlch y Moch (which is Welsh for 'pass of the pigs', and some even call it the Pig Track), and others believing it gains its moniker from its mining days, when this route was used to carry black tar – or pyg – to the copper mines. Me, I prefer to relate it to the nearby Pen-Y-Gwryd hotel (the initials spelling P-Y-G) that sits just a mile or so from the start of the path. The hotel itself is almost as legendary as the mountain; its halls full of memorabilia from the mountaineering legends who stayed there while training on Wales' mammoth mountain as a warm-up for the highs of Everest – the tallest peak in the world.

Growing up in Wales, Snowdon has always held a funny place in my heart. It's been something of a constant. Whenever I'd fly anywhere from Manchester or Liverpool, I'd often spy it on take-off or landing. When whizzing along the A55 in my days as a newspaper reporter it was my visual companion. And whenever I went for a post-hard-day's meal (a pint of tea and a mountainous chip bap – my own personal Everest) at the best walker's cafe there is (the infamous Pete's Eats at Llanberis), I would always stop for a moment at the car park above Llyn Gwynant, from where I could be guaranteed an interrupted view of Snowdon's pyramidal summit.

Now, like a distant relative, I was becoming gradually reacquainted with it through my paces, slamming my boots down into its winter coating (fallen late this year by all accounts) with determination, hoping the tread would grip adequately and keep me from sliding. The wind was surprisingly gentle on this side of the mountain. A mere sigh of a breeze, as opposed to a full-on collection of gusts.

I could see footsteps on the ground ahead of me, a sign that others had been here earlier, their tracks made lighter by a fresh falling of flakes in between their journey and mine. I pulled myself up the rocky steps, already becoming hot from the ascent. Inside my hood, with my ears well covered by my woolly earflaps, the whole process was silent, save for the gasps of my own breathing, the occasional sniff of my overactive nose and the muted squeak from the sound of my boots crunching snow.

Soon I reached the mountain pass that would take me onto the other side of the slope and deep into the belly of the interior. It's at this point that the path meets the turn-off for one of the most renowned ascents on the mountain – Crib Goch. Made from a clutter of pinnacles and jagged buttresses, the arêtes on this ridge fit all the clichés of being on a knife-edge. Many a time people do stumble, unguided and mistaken, up onto its points, and have to turn back, or call for help if they find themselves cragfast on its glacier-carved rocks.

It certainly wasn't a route that I would be tackling this time – especially not under the weight of my heavy-camping-equipment-laden backpack. I passed the signpost for Crib Goch, now fallen down under the weight of snow and high winds, and continued on my more straightforward track. Beneath me the lake of Llyn Llydaw seemed to wink at me as it came in and out of view as the clouds were blown above it. Nestled as it is on Snowdon's eastern flanks, it has a depth of around 58 metres, making it one of the deepest. Once surrounded by copper-mining activity, it now serves the purpose of helping power the hydroelectric plant down in the nearby valley of Nant Gwynant. I once stayed at a club hut that sits in the folds of the Cwm Dyli flank and remember nipping out in the early-morning light and looking up in awe at the giant pipes that tumble down the slopes carrying masses of water – they stretch up so far from there that they disappeared into the clouds that morning.

A little further on I passed a small group descending. I was, as usual, battling uphill in the opposite direction of the crowd.

'Windy up top,' one advised.

'Not a place to linger around,' said another.

'Looks stunning, though,' ventured the third.

Assessing the information I smiled and thanked them, then moved on, wondering just where I would plant my tent when I had actually battled through all this snow. It's been several years now that I've been venturing up into the hills in winter, tackling snowy peaks and waking up to a tent coated in a layer of hoarfrost. Camping in snow is like sleeping in a soundproofed chamber. Every whisper seems to be swallowed by the white; every other sense primed and heightened. It can be cold, for sure, but then it can also command some of the most incredibly clear night skies, the stars stretching on like salt granules scattered over a black napkin. It can bring with it a few extra challenges, of course – frozen ground is, after all, not the easiest to drive a tent peg into. That was a problem for later, though, I reasoned, and continued to battle onwards and upwards.

Something in the snow caught my eye – its orange colouring alien in all this white. I picked it up – a timing chip made for the lace of a training shoe that must have come loose. This mountain is famous for its trail runs – indeed, the record time to run the track from summit to town in the annual Snowdon Race is a miniscule 40 minutes. I remember once coming here in another winter – not unlike this one – reaching the top triumphantly after a long-drawn-out battle with a cornice near its summit, my face flushed with pride. I was congratulating myself on my first time leading myself and a friend on a winter walk to the summit, feeling fairly self-satisfied with our achievement, when I heard the cry of 'Good morning' pipe out from the other side of the summit cairn. I watched in disbelief as a man dressed in nothing but a thin vest, a teeny tiny pair of red shorts, a pair of socks and some flimsy-looking trainers, ran past smiling, his skin marbled from the cold, yes, but otherwise looking comfortable as he strode with giant, bold leaps past me and down the Llanberis Path. Today it seemed a similar person was out somewhere on the snowy trail.

Placing the device in my pocket I continued, nodding to a couple who told me they had decided to turn back, being ill-equipped for the conditions. A little later I reached a family. The father, clad in a fleece jacket and Gore-Tex waterproof outer layer had the look of a man unsure of his next move, the teenage kids bored by his indecisiveness, the youngest shivering from the cold – they were all dressed merely in thin jackets, jeans or trackie bottoms, and trainers.

'Excuse me, but how much further is it to the summit?' the father asked me, mustering a hopeful smile.

I pulled out my map – a map I feel I never really need on a peak I know as well as this one – its path as familiar to me as the lines on my own palms – and showed him our then position. We were still another good kilometre from the part where the Miners Track joined with ours, and another couple of kilometres still from the summit ridge – all including many metres of ascent.

'Hmm, well, about an hour and a half at least, maybe even a couple of hours depending on conditions,' I said diplomatically.

'Oh,' he mumbled, looking disheartened, 'that's not what it looks like on the map.'

I fought the urge to tell him that it was exactly what it looked like on the map if you knew how to read one properly, but instead ventured some advice.

'Perhaps you've walked enough today, there's more snow forecast and you've still got a chance to head back to the car.'

'But won't the restaurant be open?' he enquired, 'it's the Easter holidays and I thought it always opened during the Easter holidays,' he persisted.

Snowdon is a mountain that seems to divide many people. Some are frustrated by one of its oldest man-made features – a train. Opened in 1896, the rack-and-pinion track transports passengers nearly 8 kilometres up, right to within a few metres of the summit itself. It deposits them in the warmth and convenience of modern toilets, hot food and coffee, as well as selling them souvenir T-shirts that boast that the wearer has made it to the top of Mount Snowdon. Opening around Easter each year, and staying open till around October, it attracts a huge number of visitors to the summit every year – making it one of the most ascended peaks in Britain, and also one of the most avoided by hardened hill-lovers due to those same crowds.

'No, that's a weather-dependent attraction,' I advised the man. 'It never opens when there's still snow around the summit, and certainly not when there's as much snow around as this,' I gestured to our calf-deep covering of snow.

By this point his eyes had glazed over a little. I had not told him something that he cared to hear. Then one of his teenage daughters spoke up.

'Can we go? Can we go back P-L-easssse!' she emphasised.

'If you do decide to push on, do make sure you eat something before climbing onto the summit ridge,' I advised. 'You'll need all the energy you can get, because, by all accounts, it will be really windy – make sure you put on your layers then too,' I added.

'But we don't have any snacks,' he said.

I made my excuses and began to move forward, leaving him with his decision to be made. Several minutes later I dared a glance back and with relief saw the party making their way back down. It's certainly not that I don't want people to come to the wild places that I love, it's just that I want people to come and enjoy them for the right reasons – not just because they had them down on the school holiday 'to do' list when they booked a break to Wales and decided to try to stick to that list no matter what the weather dictated. Having seen many a youth group forced to 'enjoy' the outdoors in heavy and unwieldy clothing, having watched my brother grow up doing the Duke of Edinburgh Award and being allowed to do an entire expedition – which he and his group finished proudly – only to be told smugly by the assessor that they were half a kilometre short and therefore would need to do it all again, I feel strongly that it's important to get younger people enjoying the pleasures of the outdoors, rather than seeing it as an unforgiving place to go and feel cold, wet, tired and dejected. My motto has been and always will be: 'Enjoy, not endure.'

Minutes later, as I turned a corner and made rather a mess of the climb around an overhanging rock, I realised I had lost the path proper, and I saw that the weather was fast closing in on me. The views of the frosty mountainsides opposite were gone, replaced with a thick veil of murky grey sky. I looked behind to see the colours of the family's clothing disappear into the mist and, ahead of me, where before I could make out the way, depressed as it was in its snowy coating, was now gone – a blank – stolen from view. I stopped temporarily, unbalanced in my now colourless scene – as though all the pigment had been drained out of the world as I knew it. For a minute I felt a panic rising in my stomach, the natural reflex when you're suddenly struck blind in a wild place. My breathing began to quicken and I gulped hard to try to calm myself. I steadfastly placed my ice axe in the snow and decided to wait it out. Reaching into my pocket I took out a sugary sweet, unwrapped it with great concentration, and shoved it in my mouth. I looked down, concentrating on my boots, the bright blue fabric contrasting spectacularly against the snow. Seconds later the clouds cleared a little, showing me at least something of my way ahead; relief swept over me in a wave of exhilaration and I began moving once more.

With each footstep I sank further into the snow, it deceiving me with its harder top coating, then sinking effortlessly as soon as I applied some weight to it. I was no longer aiming for the summit in this clag, but for the marker post where this path joined with the Miners Track, in order to confirm I was still on the correct route.

Starting from roughly the same spot as the route I was on, the Miners Track offers a more gentle start, getting walkers into the heart of things more steadily and perhaps even with a little more drama. It first passes Llyn Teyrn, a smaller lake, and almost immediately spoils from the miners' past are revealed, with dilapidated ruins of former mining buildings rising up from the grassy slopes on the right. A little further on it reaches Llyn Llydaw, where it cuts across that lake via a well-built causeway that has been there since the 1830s. More remnants of mining buildings and shaft tops can be spied, until finally the track reaches the start of a proper climb on the shores of Glaslyn, where it zigzags up to meet the Pyg Track, from which point they continue together to the summit ridge.

At their meeting point there is a post, which, for the past number of years – and with no explanation why – has been coated with pennies and other coin equivalents by walkers. Looking like some kind of medieval weapon, it stands like a rotting tooth, glistening in even the slightest glint of light courtesy of its man-made metallic adornments.

It was there I decided to stop for a breather (and possibly some chocolate), gazing down at the water of Glaslyn, which was playing a game of hide and seek in the thick snowy mist. The lake itself is home to a number of well-known folklore tales. One of the highest lakes on the mountain, though now confirmed to have a depth of just under 40 metres, it was once presumed to be bottomless – an eternal chasm chiselled deep into the rocks on an unending voyage into the abyss.

The Arthurian legend that surrounds it also intrigues me and I thought of it now as I gazed down into the eye-shaped lake – as though gazing into the soul of the mountain itself. It was into Glaslyn that Arthur's mighty sword Excalibur was thrown. I sat in the snow now, fingering my ice axe's adze and thinking what a great name that would be for an ice axe – the Excalibur. I had the whole marketing campaign mapped out in my head – the still lake trembling as an arm emerged from it's depth clasping this king among ice axes, the name 'Excalibur' exploding across the screen – the only ice axe you'll ever need – proudly made in Wales. It's an idea, I thought to myself, that I must surely patent.

But it's not only the mythical sword that is synonymous with its waters. It's also the lake where Arthur's body was placed on board a boat to be taken to the promised afterlife of Avalon. Many believed that on that fateful day Arthur's men sought out and found a cave on the slopes of the peak that rises from the lake – Y Lliwedd – where even to this day they rest in wait until they are once again needed by their master.

I doubted whether they'd care to wake again on this day. The wind began to pick up to a more biting chill as I stood up again and began creating my own zigzags on the slopes – the proper path covered too completely for me to now unearth it. I knew that on either side of this slope I needed to be careful, not only on account of the falling snow, but also on account of the old mining shafts that still lurk on the hillside.

I continued up, cutting steps in the snow with my ice axe, taking time to make sure each footstep was secure before I ventured forward to take another. The cliffs of Crib-y-Ddysgl loomed above me like something from a bad fairy tale. Their spires and dark rocks towered aloft in a flurry-like blizzard – a dragon flying among them wouldn't have seemed amiss. Those cliffs are also the site of a legend, with mythology telling us that Merlin hid the gold throne of Britain in them after we were invaded by Saxons. No real gold has ever been found, of course, but walkers like me know that on a day like today, with barely another soul around to share this ethereal scene, there's a different type of treasure to be discovered.

By the time I reached the overhanging cornice of hard icy snow at the 993-metre point the last couple of walkers were making their way down. We nodded hellos – their mouths wrapped up safely in scarves, but their eyes sparkling, betraying their smiles beneath, telling of men who had seen a frozen encased summit cast as though under the magic smell of a sorceress – and had been enchanted. I was eager to crack on myself.

Their descents and others before them had created a network of handy holds for hands and feet and I found myself scaling upwards without needing to put on my crampons. I found myself transported from the souvenir-shop-topped summit of summer into an environment way more Alpine in character. Wind blasted me in the face as I topped out, despite having a Buff neck tube pulled up over my nose; the ice was cold in the grip of my fingers, my axe held in place within the firm clutch of hardened snow.

It's no wonder that so many headed for the Alps, and even to the Himalaya, came to Snowdon's higher cliff faces to train.

Success on the summit of Everest is owed in part to this Welsh mountain, with Sir Edmund Hillary, the first man to step foot on the summit of the world's highest peak, training here for that 1953 expedition – his name is even in the book at the youth hostel at Pen-y-Pass where I left my car, and also at the Pen-Y-Gwryd hotel. But way before Hillary, one of the first recorded rock climbs in Britain took place around the northern side of Snowdon, on the rocks known as the Clogwyn Du'r Arddu. The year was 1798 and the people involved were Peter Williams and William Bingley, who were not actually out trying to conquer a rock face, but merely searching for specimens of rare plants.

In a not dissimilar tale, the first recorded summit of the mountain was also secured by a botanist, who was also more intent on capturing and recording plant life than on claiming mountaintops in his name. He was Thomas Johnson and his unplanned summit escapade took place in 1639.

It was with a similar frame of mind that I had come here on this April evening. Not to collect plants, of course – though it is still my goal to one day find the rare and fabled Snowdon lily (a plant found nowhere else in Britain) – but to just enjoy the adrenaline felt on a summit sleep.

At that moment I topped out onto the summit ridge, where a final pull of around 500 metres would take me on to its highest point. It's always an odd moment reaching this landmark, no matter what time of the year, for here is where, after enjoying what feels like the vast and wild interior of the mountain, you are faced with the tracks of the train that brings the masses to its top. Even under a film of ice they looked incongruous in this setting, like the skeleton of some man-made snake leading down into the invisible valley below. It's from that same direction that the Llanberis Path ascends to the top. Often said to be the 'easiest' route to the top (which I often take as a euphemism for the most boring), because it pulls you up more slowly and steadily than the others, in winter it takes on a more sinister character. For a little beyond where I now stood the slope takes on a decidedly convex shape near the bend above Llyn Du'r Arddu. The path itself cuts right and actually stays well away from the edge, but, once covered by snow, the temptation is to follow the easier-to-make-out tracks that swing dangerously close to the drop. One slip is all that's needed to take you sliding to a 100-metre-plus drop. Indeed, friends of mine in Mountain Rescue name it as a notorious black spot, and a place that they tend to check first when someone goes missing in winter.

Shivering as I recalled their accounts of bodies literally piling up, I turned my back to it and instead headed south towards the summit, the tracks following me as I went. The wind immediately picked up and I stepped further away from the precipice, crouching down as low as I could go and still move. My eyes filled with tears as the gusts blasted them, my nose ran uncontrollably and my lips dried out as soon as I licked them; I could feel the skin beginning to crack.

Originally, when I'd planned my night here, I had pictured setting up my tent beneath the summit trig point rocks. As I neared them now, the mist temporarily shifting to reveal them caked in a thick layer of ice, I knew it would be impossible. I battled on to take the summit, to at least touch the trig point and know I was there, but the wind fought as hard as I did. When I finally reached the stairs up to it, I had to crawl, as though offering the airstream my submission by way of payment for my prize. My penitence paid dividends and I was granted a brief reprieve from the turbulence to grasp the trig with both arms, the winter's summit reached thanks to the clemency of the weather.

Still staying as low as I could, I made my way back down the steps and instinctively made a beeline for the cafe and railway station building. Reaching the door, I saw the phrase that's etched into the rocks there, words from Welsh National Poet Gwyn Thomas: 'The summit of Snowdon: Here you are nearer to heaven.' In these conditions, with the gusts cooling the already freezing temperature to a good few degrees below it, these words were more of a truism than a literary flourish. I began to search for a spot for my tent.

The true summit was too exposed, too risky for the conditions, so I ruled that out instantly, but I was loathe to lose too much height. Anywhere near the col wouldn't do, as that too acted as a literal wind tunnel, with sporadic gusts sure to tear my tent fabric clean away from the poles. I returned to the shelter of Hafod Eryri – the name chosen for the summit cafe when it was reopened in June 2009 – and checked the door. Though not open, the section just outside it near the steps offered the best chance of protection from the elements. OK, I reasoned, it's not quite the dream result, being rescued, as it were, by a man-made structure, but, being sensible about it, I knew that it was the best I could do height-wise without putting myself in any danger.

I set about erecting my shelter, doing a balancing act between holding the tarp and inner sheet down with my feet and struggling to clip the poles together. Luckily my tent was one I was used to. I was all too familiar with the clips that don't always clip first time, knowing the eyelets that were likely to cause me the most trouble and having made a few modifications of my own to ensure that they did. Soon it was up and I immediately hoisted my backpack inside to weigh it down. With no loose ground available to secure any tent pegs, I looked around for some rocks to borrow. I placed some inside at the corners and some outside on the edges of the outer sheet to try my best to anchor it.

I blew up my inflatable camping mat – warmed a little by the effort required – and felt myself instantly lost to the euphoric feeling always experienced when I first open my down sleeping bag. I took out my flask, filled before I left with a hearty and chunky vegetable stew, and set to work on that and my sandwich, my sleeping bag draped over my legs for warmth, my down jacket slung across my shoulders for added insulation.

It's amazing how much of the wind chill a thin fabric of nylon can remove from the air. Surrounded by the concrete walls that acted as windbreaks and snuggled into my expedition gear – the heavyweight sleeping bag I had brought was one I'd used in the Himalaya – I felt perfectly comfortable. I knew I owed it in part to the structure next door – though it would have been a different story if I'd have come here a few years earlier.

When it comes to buildings, Snowdon has had a mixed relationship with them. The very first was built in 1838, pre-railway. It was erected to reward walkers with refreshments – at a price. Just seven years later, an important service was deemed to be missing and so a licence was granted allowing alcoholic drinks to be served there. Very basic accommodation was also offered – though how much better or warmer than my four-season tent was now proving I could only guess.

Of course, a little after the Snowdon Mountain Railway was finished in 1896, the railway company also wanted in on the market, so they also added concessions selling drinks and beds for the night in what must surely have rated the highest brand rivalry in the UK. This went on for the best part of 40 years, until people began to complain about the summit sprawl. And so in 1935 work was carried out to remove all the by-then-dilapidated structures and instead build a single unit that would combine railway station, rooms and a cafe to serve everybody. Designed to incorporate a flat roof as a viewing platform, reports from visitors soon indicated that the roof leaked – as is often the way with non-sloping roofs, especially ones at a height of over 1,000 metres, where the slopes are said to be some of the wettest in the British Isles.

During the Second World War the Government took over all the buildings and, effectively, the summit. In fact, walk up the Watkin Path from Bethania in the west and you can see the disused house of the slate-quarry manager, which was used as target practice by troops. Even some old barracks still remain today. Once the fighting had stopped the rooms were kept for staff use only, instead of being opened to the public again. The whole building looked worse for wear and HRH Prince Charles famously called it 'the highest slum in Wales'. In 2006 the building was demolished and the next three years were spent building the much more sympathetic stone structure seen today. Though there are still some who think that the whole mountain should have been stripped of its man-made shackles, I couldn't help but be glad of it's partial shelter now as I lay awake in my sleeping bag listening to the wind howling.

At some point I must have nodded off, made warm by the down that surrounded me, reassured by my position. My dreams were filled with some of the oddities I had read about this great mountain. The cast from *Carry on up the Khyber* were there, filming as they had in 1969 on the lower reaches of Watkin Path (a plaque on the route commemorates the filming location). Then I was inexplicably plodding my way up the Rhyd Ddu Path, watching the summit tease me from near the start, bobbing up and down as it so often does, refusing to get any closer until suddenly I was there. Next came the gold hunters seeking out Merlin's legacy in the cliffs, whom I was fiercely trying to stop from going any further. Finally I watched in horror as the people of the Conwy Valley took their youngest, prettiest girl and left her on the riverbank to try and tempt the monster that lay in wait within the depths of the river there. When it emerged, scaled and dragon-like in my subconscious, they took it off and trapped it in Glaslyn, right below where I now slept.

I awoke with a start, the muddle of my memories starting to dissipate as though a snow cloud. I looked about me and noticed that my tent door was flapping uncontrollably, the zip ripped open by the wind. Reluctantly I unravelled myself from the heat of my sleeping bag and resecured it shut. I looked at my phone to see that it was a little past 1 a.m., still a while to go before my night would be finished. I lay restless for a while, my hands still cold from the outside air. I searched for my thin liner gloves in the pocket of my bundled-up jacket and shoved my hands in them, blowing on them with my wet breath in an attempt to warm them up.

I may not have felt the most comfortable that anyone has felt during an overnighter but I smiled to myself as more snow beat against the walls of my tent. I was the highest person in Wales, and indeed England, that night, perched among the summit rocks. I fell asleep once more, first dreaming of the giant that King Arthur is said to have destroyed, and who is said to lie under the summit of the massif I was sleeping on now – in fact, that's where Snowdon's Welsh appellation Yr Wyddfa (tumulus) comes from, referring to the mounds of earth that make up the old grave. Then I imagined the whole mountain itself forming from a huge volcano, shooting plumes of grey ash high into the air and forming its lower banks and flanks with its lava. Finally, I imagined myself looking out from the summit and (somewhat impossibly) spying the top of Ben Nevis, the highest peak in the UK – it was at that point I re-awoke.

At first I didn't move, didn't check the clock on my phone, though I could tell from the light that dawn was beginning to break outside. Instead, I lay there thinking for a minute about my dream. I then thought about the night I planned to spend on Ben Nevis, notoriously home to some of the most extreme weather in the whole of Britain, and shivered. I also worried about how I would sleep on Scafell Pike, with all its sharp rocks strewn across the summit. But then I thought about this night, about my journey to the roof of Wales. It had been a real wander back into the histories and legends that surround this peak, a peak I had known all my life but often taken for granted. My sleeping version of a three peaks challenge was hardly conventional, but at least it would give me time to appreciate these three mountains in more depth than I could on any other 3 Peaks Challenge that currently existed. I would really get to know each of them in a way that those who just stand on their summits and touch their trig points never will. Though the idea of a set challenge had seemed a shallow one when I started, I now realised with a growing pleasure that it was actually enabling me to get closer to some places I'd never thought to linger at before.

With that happy notion going through my head my eyelids began to feel the heaviness of sleep once more, and I allowed my wild dreams to return to me.

CHAPTER FIVE

SCAFELL PIKE

My eyes were stinging. Sweat had begun to drip in sporadic globules down my forehead and find its way down past my brows and into the corners of my eyes. Everything about me seemed too hot. My feet were damp in my walking socks, despite me having switched to a lightweight mid-boot, as opposed to my usual chunky but comfy leather offerings. My pack was as light as it could be and still an unflattering V-shaped patch of perspiration formed on the back of my T-shirt. I'd scraped back my hair into a loose ponytail, but still several strands had managed to work themselves free and cling needily to my neck, making me hotter still.

It was a far cry from the bleak winter scene just a few months earlier when I had begun my challenge to camp on the highest peaks of Wales, England and Scotland. Since then life, it seemed, had got in the way. With work and family responsibilities greeting me on my return from Snowdon, my challenge had been put on indefinite hold, and my Go Bag had undergone some kind of spring hibernation, relegated to my cupboard under the stairs. The mountains and my wild camping had become merely a sentence scrawled excitedly on a scrap of paper, which I had steadfastly attached to my fridge as a constant 'to-do list' reminder.

Only during a brief reprieve in August did I finally get the chance to do anything about it again. One day, after a particularly manic week ticking off chores, I reached a happy moment that comes very rarely, when I realised with a sense of teenage-like glee that I had done everything needed of me. Sure, I would have more responsibilities piled upon me in the next few days, but for one night I was free. Without telling a single soul of my plans – perhaps wildly irresponsibly but completely enjoyably – I jumped in my car and headed north, bound for the Wasdale Valley and England's highest mountain.

My way up the M6 had seemed to whizz by in an outburst of childish excitement. I had been car-singing so loudly to some truly awful music that by the time I reached the turn-off for the Lakes I could barely speak to the attendant at the petrol station without croaking.

Quite coincidentally, at the same time as my escape, Cumbria was blessed with some particularly favourable weather conditions. As I made my way up and over the mountain passes nothing could dampen my mood. The fells stretched out all knobbly and friendly without a single cloud in sight. The motorcyclists tore their way through the bends of the roads as carefree as I did in my little car; even the cyclists seem to wave cheerily as I passed them – nothing could go wrong, it seemed.

I reached the last leg of my drive, making my way up through the westernmost villages of Lakeland, wishing I could call this place home – then reminded myself that, for the night at least,

I would. I began the glorious meander alongside the shore of Wast Water.

No matter how many times I make the journey into this part of the Lake District National Park, I always stop when I reach this point. It doesn't seem to matter that at home I literally have a dozen memory cards full of shots of the peaks here, sitting at the head of the perfectly calm, mirror-like lake, looking majestic and oil-painting perfect – I always think I need more. It's normally after the first bend that it happens. I don't think I will stop, remembering all the aforementioned memory cards, but then, just as I'm about to pass a prime piece of parking real estate, I give in to my inner voice saying, 'It has NEVER looked this good'. I screech dangerously over to the bay and then leap out of the car with whatever camera or phone or picture-taking apparatus I happen to have with me at the time. I start snapping away like a woman possessed, each time thinking that this will be the last time I do this because I now have the best shot imaginable... until the next time.

This time was to be no different. I played out the exact scenario above, this time scaring a resting sheep with my antics, which I felt guilty about for all of 30 seconds and then got distracted by the view once more. It's not just me that rates this particular spot, I can assure you. A few year's ago it was actually voted Britain's Best View and it's a hard one to argue with – though there are many others that I would rate up there alongside it.

After taking at least another 20 photos – how we coped in the days before mammoth-capacity memory cards I'll never understand – I continued on my way to Wasdale Head. At the end of the valley I parked my car by some recently completed public toilets. They never used to be there but the need arose on account of the scores of Three Peakers that come here every year.

The National Three Peaks Challenge is one that sees walkers aim to complete summit ascents of the highest mountain in each of Scotland, England and Wales in a single 24-hour period, including driving time between the climbs. In my view, it has little to do with enjoying the beauty of the mountains, or the solitude and thinking space that being high on these hills can afford. To me, it's a rush up some places that should be savoured rather than passed by in a blur. Don't get me wrong, getting people to visit these places is important, but I personally don't see the point of doing them as that kind of a race.

The way most people begin the challenge is how I did, at Snowdon, setting out from Pen-y-Pass. They rush up to the summit and, presumably with barely a glance at the view, rush straight back down, where they jump into a car and eat as they make their way to Scafell Pike. Usually reached in the late evening or early hours of the morning, the little hamlet of Wasdale is next on their tick list, as it is the shortest (albeit steepest) route to the top of the mountain from there. They stumble out of the car – usually half asleep – and have a tendency to litter and (by some accounts) crap in the car parking area at the foot of the village before making their way to the summit by the light of their head torches – usually having done no other night walking before in their lives. On their way down many often bulk up on snacks, when wrappers are discarded either by mistake or by ignorance, and then any more 'toilet requirements' are taken care of before they make the last mad dash to Scotland, where they summit Ben Nevis.

Having talked to locals in all three locations, I know that Wasdale is by far the hardest hit. Unlike in Snowdonia, where residents tend to stay the night before and bulk up on a pub meal, or Fort William, where they celebrate post-challenge with a night in a hotel or B&B and give business to a local hostelry to toast their achievement, in Wasdale it literally is a fly-by-night visit with no money going back into the local economy and the volunteer-run Mountain Rescue team frequently getting called out to help those who have lost their way. It's the reason I never have done the challenge in the way that most people have. I once did the Three Peaks Challenge using public transport, enjoying a meandering route that took about a week, and I was of course in the process of doing it again now, this time round taking the time to sleep and linger at the tops rather than racing about between them. I wanted my 3 Peaks Sleeps Challenge to be something I could remember.

I first went to the Wasdale Head Inn for something to eat. Even those not staying the night on a mattress should go and check it out for its history alone. Much like the Pen-Y-Gwryd hotel in Snowdonia, it's steeped in mountaineering legend. Even to this day the likes of Sir Chris Bonington and the local Mountain Rescue team make something of a pilgrimage here on New Year's Day for a tipple.

I walked in and ordered the stodgiest meal I could find on the menu, along with a glass of some locally brewed ale. I spent my time looking at the memorabilia in the form of old ice axes and crampons that adorned the walls and imagined some of the tales of daring and near misses that must have been shared in the years preceding my visit.

The place was busy despite it being only early evening. By the bar a man sat alone nursing a pint, his hands rough and cracking, those of someone who spends much time in the extremes of the outdoors. To my right a table was crammed with excited twenty-somethings who had made an ascent of Scafell Pike earlier that day and were goading one of their members for getting scared on Lord's Rake – a rollercoaster of a splintered rock-coated route that connects the highest mountain, Scafell Pike, with the subsidiary peak known as just Scafell. Behind them was a couple, probably checked in to one of the higher-class rooms away from the main establishment, here to enjoy a romantic escape, no doubt, rather than to use the place as a base for limit-crossing escapades. In the other corner more friends – a group of men in their forties – colluded and argued over an outspread OS map of the surrounding fells. The hotly debated topic was their ascent route for tomorrow – as yet undecided.

More heads filled the spaces, a constant trickle of visitors despite the far-flung location. I sat and absorbed it all until, looking at the clock on the wall, I noticed it was past 8 p.m. With a 2-hour walk still ahead of me, it was time for me 'to head up to bed'.

After collecting my bag from the car I first made a detour to the nearby church – it's become something of a habit for me to do this. Although I knew it would not be open, I walked through the gate and into the small graveyard that surrounds it. Most people feel uncomfortable in a graveyard, but I always feel a sense of peace. I walked around the building, paying heed to the names of those that sleep here for eternity under the shadow of Scafell Pike. I took in the mountain views that surround the churchyard on all sides. As last places to lie at rest go, this certainly takes some beating.

Before I left, I made my way to the last window that faces south. I could just about see the little etching on the glass inside and the carved wooden beam that says 'I will lift up mine eyes unto the hills'. With that, I set my course for Scafell Pike.

Standing at 978 metres, Scafell Pike may not have the stature of Snowdon, but it certainly still has the character. Looking at it topographically from its summit, it seems to spin, fan-like, into the radial peaks that spill either side of it. So confusing to the naked eye is its summit and subsidiaries that for years it was in fact thought that the neighbouring peak of Scafell (no Pike) was the highest, and that the Pike had been added later to indicate a secondary top. Also, collectively with other nearby peaks, often they were referred to as simply 'The Pikes' and people would walk not really knowing (or perhaps caring) which really was the truest high point.

I walked up in the warmth of a summer's evening, having the whole place to myself. I was heading for the col at Mickledore, a broad but rocky ridge that connects the aforementioned Scafell with Scafell Pike like a stony cuff. The whole mountain was bathed in the orange half-light that comes pre-sunset. The hills opposite, out of the shadow cast by the ridge I was on, seemed to be filtered in a ginger hue, as though the whole world had now been turned auburn in the light.

I worked up a sweat doing the first bit, around to the giant boulders where the path flattens out before climbing again. Despite the dimming daylight it was still warm, the boulders themselves hot to touch, acting like storage heaters radiating warmth – even sitting on one of them seemed to warm me too much – it certainly was not winter any more.

In recent years, due to the sheer numbers of the determined Three Peakers that plough this landscape, they have put in a new path. From the point where I was standing it continues on till it lines up perfectly with the summit, then it climbs in a series of zigzags all the way to the rocky top. The way I was heading up was more of a classic, though. Eroded by footfall, but somehow fainter because of the falling rocks and scree slopes, it cuts up from the boulders and directly onto the loose stuff, before topping out at Mickledore. From there it's a rough path, often marked by tiny marker stones that lead to the much-desired trig point.

I headed up confidently, having ascended this route many times before. The higher I went, the more I could make out the new path in the distance. Only recently bedded, it glimmered almost white, like a motorway scarring the hills. On first impression it was a bit of an eyesore, but I knew that it needed to be there, to keep the people who did not come to enjoy these aged mountain passageways, but merely to get from A to B, on the right track, and to stop the endless call-outs to Mountain Rescue.

The rocks sounded like they were exploding under my boots, each footstep loud on the empty slope. I continued up, stopping every now and then to wipe the moisture from my brow. From my vantage point now I could see into the valley, and the stillness of Wast Water made it appear as though I was looking down on a double valley, with everything reflected perfectly inside it. I thought about how I always made a second stop on my way home to take yet another photo, and thought about the people who no doubt would be heading home now and doing just that, and how these mountains would be appearing on Facebook and Twitter any minute now, with me an invisible soul clinging to their edges.

I carried on up, reaching the scree; here I edged my way up slowly, the ground every few steps almost shifting back down to where I had been before taking those same steps. From here I could make out the undulating corridor that is Lord's Rake and for a moment, just for the thrill of the journey it offered, I wished that Scafell was indeed the highest peak and then I would get to traverse Lord's Rake to reach its summit. For the first time I felt a pang of resentment, being bound by my own rules on this preset challenge.

Right at the top of one of the steepest undulations sits a large rock that many years ago fell off one of the many gullies that line the walkway. It came to rest quite precariously at the top and so far there it remains, though at any minute it could start rolling. It was such a worry that for a while the local authority asked people not to use the route, but now it appears to be open once more, time making the likelihood of a fall perhaps lessen in people's minds.

I reached Mickledore and with a quick heave clambered on top of it to survey my new high. To my left the route up to Scafell Pike rose in a higgledy-piggledy mass of splintered stones, each covered with crampon scratches left in the many winters it had seen. To my right sat Scafell and a slab of rock that had seemingly fallen against it at an angle, creating a doorway to a very difficult route to the top. I knew it because I'd attempted it once before with a friend. We had come here with ropes and protective gear and he, being the experienced climber, had gone first to make it safe and assess the conditions.

Being no climber – I blame it on having wide hips and no upper-body strength whatsoever – I had been unashamedly nervous about it. That day we'd set off from a wild camp down in Great Moss, on the Eskdale Valley side of the peak. We'd camped beneath some of the giant stones that are seemingly littered across the riverbanks and had risen early to get a head start on our goal. We'd scrambled first up a waterfall to get onto the main path and then steeply made our way up towards the col.

'Fat man's agony, they call it,' said my friend as he checked my harness and tied me in. 'So called because, well, because you'll soon see for yourself.'

On that particular day we had not enjoyed the warm and dry conditions I found myself in now. It, too, had been in August, but that August had been a particularly damp one and I had been forced to squeeze on all my climbing gear over the top of my waterproofs. When I approached the aforesaid rocky opening and stepped up onto the rock within, I instantly understood where the sobriquet had come from. I thought I was stuck fast.

'Don't panic, just push on,' came my friend's voice from the other side of the rock and I had persevered to pop out onto a flattened but slightly downwardly inclining ledge – the start of the route known as Broad Stand.

That particular crag I knew very well. I'd researched it in previous years and knew that the rather squeamish man who had first encountered it was an English poet on the descent rather than the ascent. He had made it, but waxed lyrical about its perils for many more adjectives than had been required. He wasn't the only one to be caught out by it, though. From the ground it doesn't look that far or, indeed, that dangerous. But looks can be a funny thing in the mountains. The safest line up usually sits on the very outside, where there are plenty of ledges big enough to stand on and lots of holes to grip with the hands and place the feet on. But due to our inbuilt need for self-preservation, heading out to airy and exposed ledges does not come naturally. So if we can avoid them, we will. On that particular climb, we instead seek solace in a route that cuts up using the two adjoining rocks, which create something of a right angle. The problem is that there aren't adequate holds for all but the most skilful of climbers, so if you fall or change your mind and try to jump down, you find yourself landing on that same sloping area of rock that I had been standing on, building momentum and unable to stop.

It was with a slight sense of relief, then, that on that fateful August afternoon my friend decided to call it off, due to rain the previous couple of days forming something of a mini cascade down it further up. I tried to act disappointed but couldn't quite wipe off my face the gigantic grin of a person who has just narrowly escaped facing their fear.

Now I gazed over to that same rock, pleased that no such decision awaited me today – my friend would have definitely forced me up there in these conditions, as he had on many a climb before.

The col at Mickledore is a funny place. Nestled in between the piles of rocks sits a Mountain Rescue stretcher box, complete with supplies to help mend a wounded walker, in addition to the aforementioned stretcher. I know climbers who have slept in or under these containers so that they would be close to the climbing routes that line up alongside

Lord's Rake early the next morning. I also had the vague recollection of being here with a mountain guide who had said that back in the day they even kept emergency morphine in them, but then had to remove it as too many addicts got wind of it and were purposely heading to the mountains to get hold of it. How true this last fact was I don't know for sure, but I did have to offer a certain admiration for those so determined to get their fix that they would literally scale the highest mountain in England for it.

I stopped there to take some water and peered down into the Eskdale Valley once more. From this point I could see the Great Moss area intersected with streams and pockets of water. The light was starting to fade, turning the valley floor from green into a hazy blue. Seldom visited by the Wasdale crowds, down there everything seemed still, as though frozen in time.

I remembered that, on the same day I was granted a reprieve from the impending Grade 3 scramble on Broad Stand, I hadn't got off completely scot-free. We'd gone on to summit Scafell, then on the way down we traversed an expansive boulder field to get back to the tent more quickly, so that we could walk out that day and have a good pub meal and pint to celebrate. I had been doing alright at first, chatting away as we went, not really worried or concerned about what I was doing, but then the boulder I had my right foot firmly on began to slip as I lifted my left leg. I knew I was going to go over, could sense the impending tumble, and then did perhaps one of the stupidest things possible – I reached out my hand for a rock to stabilise myself with. As a result, I not only flipped and bounced with quite a force, I also heaved a heavy rock onto myself at the same time. It all happened very quickly and by the time my friend reached me I was already beginning to feel hotter with embarrassment than pain. He pulled off the boulder that I was still clutching under my left arm and asked if I could feel anything. I attempted to get up and only then realised how much I was aching. Luckily my head hadn't been hit, but my base-layer top was ripped, my elbow was bruised and bleeding, and my trousers were also cut open. My leg was an interesting mix of purple and blue shades, not to mention warm with the flow of blood. All that was superficial, though. The real pain came when I tried to walk, my joint twingeing and aching with each step I took.

Almost as imprudent as my fall, we'd left our first aid kits back with everything else we'd stashed under the stones, so I had to make the half-hour wobbly walk back before I could tend to my bleeding. I was fine, of course, just a little shaken, but I remember the defiance I felt once I got back to base to get myself out of the valley unaided. I wouldn't allow my friend to carry my backpack for me, nor would I allow him to take any more items than was his fair share. I believe that if you do that, it's a slippery slope down to not wanting to venture into these places again. If you got yourself in, you can get yourself out – it's all a mind game.

Much like my experience of the river crossing in Glencoul, where I had literally got out of my depth, I felt good that I'd rescued myself on the slopes of Scafell. I arrived at the hostel further down the valley that night aching all over, tired and sore, wet and cold, but as I lay in my bunk bed, the sheets hurting just by resting on some of my bruises, I couldn't help but beam. I had got out – all by myself.

As I began to head up to the summit of Scafell Pike now, loneliness was certainly something I was craving over crowds.

But I wasn't to get it immediately. I met a surprised-looking couple sitting on a rock near the trig point. As they were in no apparent rush to leave and my belly was rumbling despite the calorific and carb-heavy meal I'd sunk just hours beforehand at the Wasdale Head, I took out my camping stove and began boiling some water for a cup of soup.

Almost in reply the husband of the couple whipped out his flask and offered his wife a hot drink. She didn't look impressed. 'Don't we have something more like that?' she interrogated, gesturing at the pasta-filled sachet I was pouring into the steaming liquid.

A little after 10 p.m., in the remaining light, the couple left and I had the plateau all to myself, finally. Covered in a mass of rocks, Scafell Pike is, in geological terms, described as being part of the Borrowdale Volcanics. Said to be formed mainly through weather, i.e. rain, wind and frost, it's a difficult space to know just where is safest to put up an inflatable mattress.

Not only has Scafell Pike been the subject of great debate over its height – stood at the top trig point now, I looked east to Scafell and thought without question that the latter appeared to be at least a few metres higher – but mention its name to many hillwalkers and often they'll correct you in pronunciation and spelling too. The peaks were originally printed on the map as Sca-Fell Higher Top and Sca-Fell Lower Top – the name of Scafell Pike wasn't given till around the early 1800s, after they were both measured and what is now Scafell Pike was found to be higher. But even the pronunciation then got complicated. Some people called it Scawfell (with a very pronounced 'aw') Pike as recently as the 1920s, rather than the 'Scar-fell Pike', or sometimes 'Scaf-ell Pike', sound more common today. Some walkers still insist the 'aw' is the way to go and many will argue it till they are blue in the face – so be careful to pick your battles.

Whatever the correct pronunciation of this once-subsidiary but now major peak, it doesn't detract from it being one hell of a mountain.

I wandered around for a while, checking inside the remains of the old huts that are strewn across the whole summit for possible sleeping cavities. The main summit itself was out of the question, what with the rocks, but I found an alternative on the south summit, where a thick carpet of moss made for a makeshift mattress. I had come equipped with a bivvy bag for this one, intent on slipping myself behind one of the former shelters, but this spot would do nicely.

As I set about arranging my bed I gazed out to see the coastal town's lights beginning to pop on one after another. From my high vantage point I could make out the summits of Coniston Old Man and Great Gable, and over the Solway Coast into the Southern Uplands of Scotland. I could even see over to Wales and Snowdonia, as well as Northern Ireland – it seemed too perfect a view to sleep through.

I certainly was not the first to ever sleep on its summit. In fact, the teams of Ordnance Survey crew who lovingly mapped these wonderful British Isles had quickly realised that the views from here were perfect tools for calculating triangulations. In 1826 they took up their positions on the tops of Scafell Pike, Snowdon and Slieve Donard (the highest peak in Northern Ireland) to measure the angles and distances between the three and so work out the relative position of Britain to Ireland. As their work relied on being able to actually see all three landmarks, they often set up summit camps to wait for the right weather conditions. The Principal Triangle that was formed became an important tool in mapping and, as I climbed into my sleeping bag and bivvy that night, I wondered if those men had ever realised just what a large part their wild nights out under the stars would one day mean to walkers and wild campers like me who, in the many years that followed, would rely on them to carry them safely through these high places.

With thoughts of campfires and cheery banter going through my head I quickly drifted off to sleep, thinking how lucky I was with the weather and to get this experience all to myself.

Footsteps, coming fast and decidedly, stirred me. I opened my eyes, but for a split second worried that they were still actually closed, as it was still so dark overhead, save for a few stars. I turned my head and gazed over to the trig point. I'd been doing this long enough to realise that what I was hearing wasn't the sound of a misguided sheep or active night rabbit. No, these footsteps were definitely not from wildlife.

I fought for a few seconds to decipher what I was seeing, before my eyes caught up with my ears. Human. The shape of a figure seemed to be coming straight towards me, their head torch unmistakable, blinding me with its bright stroke in this darkened plateau. I held my breath quickly, not wanting to give my position away. What was this person doing here so late? I wondered. Then, as he merely touched the trig point and got out his phone to take a selfie, it suddenly made sense – Three Peaker – of the walking, rather than sleeping, variety. It was August; the weather was perfect, prime time for the challenge-obsessed to make their voyage north. Without any more time to soak in his surrounds he was off and I turned back over to sleep, in despair.

Just as I was about to drop off again I heard more footsteps
– this time they were multiple. I turned over to see a group of
four stumble wearily to the trig point then carefully unfold a
sheet that stated they were doing this for charity – in the pallid
scene I could not work out which one. They dutifully took
turns in taking photos, before folding their banner away and
leaving by the same route they had arrived.

Minutes later it happened again and this time, when the
walkers had dashed off, I got out of my sleeping bag and pulled
on my walking trousers and boots. I made my way cautiously
to the edge of the summit to gaze down into Wasdale. There
below, a procession of head-torch lights made their way up
along the motorway-like path I had seen earlier that evening.
Some were heading down into the darkness, with others
heading upwards towards me. Some were sticking to the path
rigidly, others seemed to fumble about, confused among the
rocks about which way they were indeed heading.

The summit of Scafell Pike was actually gifted to the
National Trust nearly 100 years ago by the landowner, one
Lord Leconfield. In a decent move for an aristocrat, he offered
it in memory of 'The men of the Lake District who fell for
God and King, for freedom, peace and right in the Great War
1914–1918'. This was yet another peak connected with our
war efforts. I felt sure, when he handed it over all those years
ago, he never thought it would act as such a Mecca for this
strange breed of Three Peakers that seemed to be spread out
across it now.

Despite my misgivings about those who do the challenge,
I had to admit that from this height, looking down on this
assortment of moving lights buzzing like fireflies in the dark, it

did hold its own particularly unique beauty. It reminded me of a modern-art installation, designed to show the movement of human beings in remote places – another idea I would have to patent. It's funny how some of the best ideas come to you when you're high on a mountain summit, rather than sat at home with the luxury of pen and paper to hand.

I watched them for a while, going back for my bivvy and relocating it to beside one of the old structures so I might peer into the valley longer, mesmerised by this unnatural light show. The warmth soon got the better of me, though, and, just as I began to worry that in my current location I may inadvertently be snuggled up in one of the world's highest makeshift latrines, I fell asleep once more.

The bright rays of a muted sunrise stirred me for the final time that stay. I crawled out from the comfort of my bag and put on my shoes once more, deflating the camping mat and rolling up the rest of my camp into one big package to chuck back into my rucksack.

Another night spent high, I mused as I began to follow the trail built for the Three Peakers back down into the Wasdale Valley, tutting to myself every time I saw a discarded clump of used tissue papers, or the discarded pieces of a chocolate bar wrapper and, at one point, oddly, a single shoe in the middle of the path. I made quick work of the descent, the clouds beginning to move in as I did. It seemed the last of the summer weather was over for now. I hoped, if I did manage to also sleep on the top of Ben Nevis sometime soon and thereby complete my sleeping version of the challenge, that I might be responsible for pioneering a more 'take your time' approach to doing the National Three Peaks Challenge, a plea to others to take the time to really experience that which they seek to conquer, rather than blindly following their leader to the summits and back down. And I hoped any fellow wild campers would at least remember to take their rubbish back down with them, starting new habits for those in the wild places.

Soon I reached my car and began the drive back down south, duty-bound by some new responsibilities. The missed calls and emails on my beeping phone meant they lay waiting for me. I weaved my way alongside Wast Water, determined to change my own habit, too, while I was at it. I thought I would do it, thought I'd pass the turning without stopping, and the spell would be broken. But then at the last minute I caught sight of the peaks in my rear-view mirror and the urge took over. Once more I screeched to an emergency stop in the lay-by, yet again I grabbed my camera-phone, and once more I began snapping away at Britain's Best View. I guess some habits are hard to break.

CHAPTER SIX

BIG BAD BEN

Commitment is something I've never been the best at. In my late teens I moved through casual jobs seemingly by the weekend; in my twenties I relocated my home more times than my parents did within their whole lifetime; and, still in my early thirties, I have only just started to think that perhaps I should get my own house. My life seems to go in a cycle of: 1. Get back from adventure with no money. 2. Write about adventure to make money. 3. Use money for next adventure – then go back to 1.

I was a product of the nineties, which had immediately succeeded the depressions and recessions of the eighties, and consequently my life has never been about long-term goals. I call it my 'Pay As You Go' life, much like the phone contracts that first came out when I was in the sixth form, and which I still invested in until just a couple of years ago, when the idea of asking important contacts to look out for my phone call then ring me back when I hang up because I'm out of credit stopped looking cute and began to look a little unprofessional.

It was because of this attitude that I had faltered on my promise to finish my 3 Peaks Sleeps Challenge. After Scafell Pike life had once again put my plans on hold, and I started to wonder if I would ever actually get any further with it. And now, months on, if I was ever to complete it and follow it up with my longer and more demanding Extreme Sleeps Challenge, I knew that I needed to make a more unbreakable commitment, a reason for doing my own personal challenges that involved another person that I could let down if I didn't do it. As a journalist I needed a deadline, and as a person too busy to commit to several days in a row I needed a cause. I needed to add some pressure.

So I drafted an email several times to an outdoor filmmaker, asking if he thought my mission had any potential for him to make something of it. When he surprisingly came back with a tentative yes, with instructions to film whatever I could on my journey by myself, whenever I could, I knew I could no longer keep putting it off. The time to do this was now.

I'd already flaked off twice on my plans so far, as a result of other things cropping up. I needed to do this in one fell swoop, I decided. In one single trip, during which no excuses could stop me from seeing it through to the end. I reasoned that I needed only to sleep on Ben Nevis the once, and in doing so would complete the 3 Peaks Sleeps and also kick-start the Extreme Sleeps Challenge. So my next step was to book the time off work. With too many important things happening for at least the next six weeks I had to settle, much to my dismay, on a week in late November, just enough nights to do it – with no wriggle room.

And so, on a drizzly grey Monday, before the sun had even properly come up, my head still fuzzy from the land of dreams, I pointed the car north and put my foot down. It had begun.

Much like it is for the Three Peakers I ranted about so much earlier, I soon realised, as another hour slipped by on the same motorway, that this trip was going to involve a lot of driving. Long-distance road-tripping in Britain may sound like a misnomer, because surely in the grand scheme of things – compared to America, say – the longest continuous trip is equivalent to only traversing one US state. In Britain, though, I think we gauge driving differently. The landscapes change faster, from cities to countryside, from high fells back to concrete. And still I drove on.

Soon I knew I would cross the border into Scotland and the excitement began to rise in my belly. I looked out for all the telltale signs: the information board advising of the proximity of Gretna Green and its outlet village, which I knew I had to bypass before transition would be complete; and the 'Better Together' and 'Yes' signs that hung by the roadside, remnants from the recent vote on Scottish independence.

Then it happened, within a blink of an eye. The 'Welcome to Scotland' sign reared its head, its white cross on a blue background bursting through the grey cloud. I fumbled around at once for the video camera – suddenly remembering to try to tell part of this story visually and not just with the jumble of words in my head. I pressed 'record' just as I neared it, and then it was gone and I was wasting valuable battery life and recording time filming the backs of trucks. I quickly stopped it; this little device was already adding a new dimension to my journey.

It was still several hours later that I at last arrived in Fort William – and I was woefully underprepared. I'd watched the clock the whole time I'd been snaking my way over Rannoch Moor, checked it again as I left Glencoe, and looked mournfully at it again as I reached the last painfully slow leg along the loch's edge into town. By the time I rolled into Morrisons supermarket car park, where I needed to pick up supplies, it was past 3 p.m. and already beginning to go dark.

First things first, I thought. I needed to get a lightweight camping meal – in this challenge, with no reprieve from the elements and seven consecutive nights wild-sleeping, every gram was going to count. I walked over to Ellis Brigham and went inside to be hit with a blast of pre-cooled, air-conditioned air that I felt was working to prepare me for my night on top of The Ben. I searched everywhere for the camping meals, high and low, but found nothing at all. So I went and stood by the register and waited for someone to see what I was doing.

Sure enough the shop assistant ambled over. 'What d'you need?' he asked.

'Where are your camping meals? I can't find them anywhere,' I replied.

'Those? Well, it's winter – no real demand for them now, so I took them off the shop floor nearly a month ago – did you need one?' he looked a little taken aback by my outlandish request, regarding me curiously. Who was this odd woman looking to sleep under canvas when night falls early and the temperature regularly plummets to freezing. I was clearly not your typical camper...

'Yes, please – Wayfarer, if you can – preferably the veggie curry,' I requested as he ambled away looking confused. Though I had packed more than enough gas, I didn't want to take the risk of running out and not being able to eat, so I went for the pre-cooked, boil-in-the-bag number, to be assured of a feast.

In the supermarket things moved even slower and I mused that if things took any longer I would not leave myself enough time to actually sleep on top of the damn thing. By the time I trundled my way down into Glen Nevis, where I would actually begin my ascent of Ben Nevis, the car thermometer was reading 3°C – and it was going to get a lot colder.

I parked my car near the youth hostel, somewhere I had stayed before when I'd done my Three Peaks by public transport. The rain was still falling. I had chosen The Ben tonight, as the first sleep in my seven-night challenge, after I'd seen the forecast. As much as I'd wanted to start in the south and work my way up to end in glorious and spectacular fashion with a night as the highest person in Britain, it was not meant to be. As anyone who has climbed the mountain will appreciate, catching it in good weather is tricky, very much a gamble. In fact, during the several times I'd been up there I had never once seen a view from the top – the cloud had always engulfed me completely.

During a weather study that took place on this very mountaintop between 1883 and 1904, it was found that, between the months of November and January, it was covered by fog for 80 per cent of the time. Not only that, but over the 365 days of the year the summit saw on average 261 gales and collected over double the rainfall that Fort William below experienced in a year, or eight times that experienced in London. So when I saw a little clear-sky logo on the forecast the day before, I knew I had to head here immediately and screw the plan I had imagined from the outset.

I knew that there would definitely be snow on the summit at this time of year – there's often snow there year-round anyway – but I'd checked to see what it would be like overnight and, quite importantly, in the morning, and tomorrow looked to be the best day in the next seven.

I didn't linger at the car. I packed up what food supplies I would need and glanced over to the hostel. There I saw a group of people inside, laughing and joking, cosy and warm with their friendly conversation and clasping mugs of steaming tea – for just a split second I felt a pang of jealousy, cold as I was in the darkening night.

Then I shook it off and set off on my long walk to bed. I started across the slippery bridge that took me over the Nevis River and onto the path that leads steadfastly uphill. I crossed the stile that works to tire out your legs way too early in the climb. Rain was already in the atmosphere, a fizzle-like spray, constant but not too heavy, but under the weight of my tent, extra-warm sleeping bag, loads of snacks, crampons and an ice axe, I was already wet with sweat beneath my waterproof jacket and trousers.

Sheep were my constant companions as I went higher up; first they appeared as large white rocks that began to move around me. I still hadn't put on my head torch, trying to navigate using the last of the dying daylight. From somewhere down the valley I could hear the chug of a chainsaw. Whereas in the past this sound would have got me imagining all kinds of psycho killers on the loose in this wild valley, now it did not. I knew better, knew that it was the sound of forestry workers completing their logging duties further down the valley before clocking off. I looked at my watch. It was a little after 6 p.m.

The rumble of a tractor carrying the felled trees echoed in the dark air, and somewhere in the distance I could just about make out the edges of a rain cloud heading my way. Things were going to get rough.

I made my way higher up the giant stone steps that headed into the low-hanging cloud – so much for the predictions I'd read of a clear night. It began to fall properly now, the night; everything seemed an off-shade of blue. Every now and then I could make out the shapes of the large whiter stones that seem to glow bright against all the others on the path – almost as though they were lighting up. But still I did not put on my head torch; I was trying not to attract attention.

A little further on and the rain really came. I had been monitoring it silently for a while, ignoring the occasional drip on my face, but then it came in properly hard, heavy and cold. And all of a sudden those handy white stones I could make out before to keep leading me onwards had disappeared into the cracks of darkness. Soaked by rain, I could no longer make out the sheep. I was alone.

I continued on determined, refusing to put on my head torch, save for when the path seemed to swing sharply to my left and I could make out the shape of a man-made sign.

'Do not pass this way' (meaning the path that was straight ahead) was all it said and I turned out the light and followed the path up to my left. I knew that soon I would be at what many know as 'Half-Way Lochan'. Perched at around 570 metres above the valley floor, Lochan Meall an t-Suidhe roughly divides the ascent of this summit path into two. The track I was on has a number of names assigned to it, including the Ben Path (the Ronseal approach to path-naming), the less-than-flattering Tourist Route, and the more historical Pony Track, It was the very first path cleaved into the mountainside in 1883, made to take people up to the summit and designed with a relatively low gradient, not to help tired walkers but to enable ponies to cart up supplies to the top of the mountain.

Feeling quite pony-like myself, I stubbornly persisted onwards, still unsure of when I would reach the water and be able to celebrate a job halfway done. My eyes were beginning to feel heavier with each step, my body clearly releasing a good, strong dose of melatonin in the darkness, willing me to slip off into a wonderfully peaceful sleep.

I reached around my back to locate my water bottle, trying to shake off my body's temporary attempt at sleep. I was having to battle hard against myself, doing everything I could to stay awake. Then the fog came in.

Like a thick icy soup it seeped into the air around me, cold and unforgiving. As it touched my lips it seemed to instantly dry out, and my hands felt bitterly frozen. Freezing fog – it had to be. As I reached a flattened section of land, shaking and frozen, the wind picked up too, blasting me with Arctic-level air and lowering the temperature to well below zero. All at once I could not see. The lochan that I was so convinced was there, had seemingly disappeared, lost in a world of murk. I relented and turned on my head torch, but it didn't help. All I could see were the drops of hail in front of me forming a kind of wet, beaded curtain. All about me the path was lost, my way forward gone.

The old me might have persevered, might have continued in misery until I ran out of strength and attempted to pitch on sloping ground where I would have been heavily exposed to the breeze. But I knew what I had to do – with 700 metres still remaining between me and the summit, and the clag around me so thick I could barely make out my own hand when held in front of me, I had to call it. I was not going to make it to the summit that night. My challenge was on yet another indefinite hiatus.

I felt a twang of disappointment run through me – the admission of defeat such a bitter pill to swallow. Then I remembered the camera. I pulled it out, set it to night mode so that I became an alien-like green figure, my eyes glowing as I stared down the lens and began to talk. I explained my action and how I would try to camp and rest here for now, until the conditions improved. Justifying myself to my filming friend made me feel better about having made the decision and, instead of feeling feel bad for myself, I greeted the next task at hand head on – to find a bit of sheltered, flat, dry ground perfect for pitching a tent on.

After a few false starts towards where I thought the water was, resulting in me reaching knee-deep bogs, I continued to scout out the land. It was either too sloping or too wet, and I began to think I might have to descend a little to find somewhere suitable; then I saw it. A perfectly hollowed-out collection of rocks. Fighting with the wind I tucked my little shelter into its stony embrace and jumped inside, the chill instantly put at bay by my nylon shelter.

I made myself some food and angrily noticed that the rain had started to desist. I considered whether, after eating, I should pack everything away and make a dash for the summit, but then the rain came back harder, heavier and for much longer than last time. I snuggled down into my sleeping bag, did a few words to camera and then waited for sleep to find me, promising myself that should things improve remarkably then I would indeed set off for the summit.

Sleep did, as it turned out, find me pretty quickly. Before I realised it I was dreaming for some reason about a stag, standing proud on the mountainside, surveying his land. There he was, his antlers rising above his large eyes like some kind of skeletal crown, the fur on his chest bold and curly, his legs persistently rooted to the spot on his mountain. Then I heard a shot and watched as this majestic creature collapsed and fell to the ground.

I awoke with a shock and sat bolt upright, shaking all over. Despite the wind whistling outside and the cold turning my nose red, I felt hot, so I unzipped my sleeping bag a little. I couldn't be sure whether the shot had happened in my dream only and the dream had, therefore, in itself woken me, or if something had happened in reality and my brain had constructed an elaborate dream around it in order to startle me awake.

I lay for several minutes to see if another shot came, to confirm or deny whether I might still actually be dreaming, whether I was truly here at all. I looked at my phone's clock – I had only been out for an hour. I rested my head back against my rucksack and closed my eyes.

Silence. It woke me up with a jolt, nearly as shockingly as the gunshot had a few hours earlier. Whereas before there had been a constant battering against my tent walls, the guy lines flapping in the breeze, the whole structure around me seeming to threaten that it would at any moment fly away, everything now lay still.

I pulled on my jacket and wiggled my way out of the sleeping bag, unzipped my inner door and then the flap. My jaw dropped.

Outside I was looking up at a blanket of a thousand stars, peppering the black with granules of sparkle. It was magical. Without even pulling on my boots I went outside properly, my long johns letting in the cold early-hour air through each stitch as I stood there.

This seemed like a repayment for my restraint in calling this challenge early. It was as though the mountain had rewarded me for being sensible – nature was sending me a message and I was the only one around for miles, here on this hillock above the towns below, ready to listen.

I packed my things away as quickly as I could and got dressed. It was well below freezing, my tent was caked with a layer of hoarfrost, my boots were stuck to the outer sheet of the tent walls, meaning I had to peel them off it. I wanted to catch up on lost time and set about climbing further up the old pony track, watching the sun begin to rise above the hills beyond. How I wished I'd been able to start the day on the top. The higher I climbed, the sooner I realised with glee that I was in fact witnessing my very first cloud inversion, a phenomenon that happens when the cloud line falls below the highest peaks, meaning that those lucky enough to be up high – aka me – find themselves standing above them, watching other hilltops peek through the fluffy white blanket like islands on the sea.

The higher I got, the better the inversion got. The sun beat down on me, defrosting my frozen kit. My face was warmed twice, by my exertion and by the rays of the sun. I was agog. As I reached the last of the zigzags proper, I heard voices and looked below to see the specks of red that signified some walkers were several hundred metres below me on this same track. They must have started their journey particularly early.

Standing at 1,344 metres high, Ben Nevis is by far the highest peak in the British Isles, though for many years it was thought to be the less easily accessible Ben Macdui in the Cairngorms to the east. Records show that Ben Nevis was first climbed – as Snowdon was – by a botanist who was collecting specimens in the area. The year was 1771, the month was August, but try as I might I can't verify whether or not he got good weather when he 'summited' – the chances are that he didn't. His name was James Robertson and he was from Edinburgh. A few years after he did it a geologist by the name of John Williams also made the ascent. Back then it was not considered to be the highest peak, so it was of little interest to people. However, in 1847 those all-knowing guys at Ordnance Survey measured and confirmed its place as the highest thing in the British Isles. As such, it is now one of the most climbed mountains in the entire country, with recent guesstimates quoting a number in excess of 100,000 for total number of ascents each year, 75 per cent of which are made on the path I was now utilising.

With that many people desperate to get to the top it, it is unsurprisingly the scene of a fair few call-outs to Mountain Rescue. The tricky part comes at the section I was now beginning to traverse, the large and expansive summit plateau, a 100-acre (or 40-hectare) mass of stones and splintered rocks, not to mention a few man-made spoils. The shape of it is what causes most of the drama. Moulded like a giant kidney bean, the problem comes after significant snowfall, when the section of the mountain that indents to make the kidney-like shape becomes covered and banked up with a giant cornice. In bad weather it all looks like one giant, flat football pitch, which means the unwary could easily stumble onto the cornice, where nothing but fresh air sits beneath the snow, meaning a fall to their certain death.

The best way to avoid this one-way ticket down is to take two compass bearings from the summit trig point in order to navigate across it safely. However, as this is the biggest, highest peak, it undoubtedly attracts many people for whom taking a compass bearing is the equivalent of being asked, when caught on a plane with a sick pilot, to fly it to a safe landing. So it was decided by the local Mountain Rescue team at the end of the 1990s to put up marker posts on the summit plateau to help people safely descend in bad weather. Cue the uproar from the purist hill folk, who complained that it was unethical because not only did it hamper stunning views of the natural landscape, it also encouraged unprepared souls to come here, as there was now a perceived 'easy way' out of trouble.

Looking across the plateau now those old posts are long gone. It wasn't the Mountain Rescue team who removed them, but the climbers who objected to them. Now what stands there instead is a series of huge stone cairns that mark the last kilometre of the Pony Track, placed here six years ago and as of now still standing.

As much as I would love to take the moral high ground of the purist, I cannot. I like these cairns, find them reassuring. If they were on any other mountain I might object, but this is one peak that begs to be climbed often by people without the experience, so let them have this one, I tell the protestors. Let them make this one safe. I've been here in winter myself and noted how often, after a heavy period of snow, only the very tips of these giant markers can be seen. Today, under less than a foot's coating, they stood higher than me. I remember being here in cold fog, setting my compass and feeling relieved when one by one these handy aids presented themselves to me, confirming my bearing.

The sun was moving in and out of the clouds that day, offering me occasional glimpses of the trig point. I didn't need the cairns, but I noted just how high they were on this visit, too early in the season to be of use yet, the cornice not yet built up on the edge. Still, I walked slowly, happy to be the only one up there so far, enjoying the crunch each footstep was afforded as it broke fresh snow beneath its tread.

Slowly the remains of the old observatory tower came into view. Built in 1883 this summit laboratory came about as part of a growing global trend to place observatories in high places of the world to study weather at altitude. Before it was given the go-ahead, a meteorologist called Clement Wragge ascended it every day to make recordings of the weather, laying the groundwork for the Scottish Meteorological Society to get their station approved. It was manned full time for a total of 21 years until its closure in 1904 due to funding cuts, and its existence led to the pitching of the pony track and the corresponding allure for people to ascend its summit. So popular was a visit to the top of the world there that in 1894 many proposals were put forward to erect a train track to take tourists to its summit – like the one on Snowdon. Thankfully, permission was never obtained.

Now the observatory stands as a mere collection of bricks and empty window openings. As controversial as man-made structures inevitably are on mountains, there is a part of me that would have very much liked to have been stationed up here in the early 1900s, to have had my address as 1 Ben Nevis,

Fort William. The wilderness lover inside me is, of course, pleased that it no longer functions, is thankful to see that year upon year the mountain is slowly reclaiming it, pulling down its door frames, sending once-thick walls into piles of building rubble and, in winter, often covering the whole thing with a thick layer of snow.

Whether its erection was right or wrong, the thorough set of data recorded by the team over that two-decade period is still used today as a valuable tool to predict climates in mountain environments. And it was here in 1894 that a member of staff by the name of C. T. R. Wilson first saw a Brocken spectre, which happens when the sun casts a halo-like shadow on top of the observer. This led him to create his own cloud chamber back at sea level to try and better understand the marvel, which in turn resulted in his visualisation of particle tracks, allowing physicists to see the activity of the subatomic world for the first time.

I walked among the ruins, taking a minute to stop at the memorial that sits among them to remember those who died in the Second World War. I took off my glove to feel the cold rock under my fingertips and winced as the chill stung at my skin.

Alongside the remains of the observatory is a small summit shelter propped up on a tower of rock. Opposite is the trig point perched on another, similar, tower of rocks, with steps cut into the back of it. I remember coming here in April one year, the snow so deep that the towers were non-existent. Snow alone had spanned the distance from the trig to the shelter, all at the same high level. I went first to stand on top of the cairn and look out over my surrounds. As the highest person in Britain at that moment I had, for the first time in my life, an uninterrupted view of the landscape, the wind helpfully blowing the swirling mist away.

From Ben Nevis' summit there is no higher ground until western Norway, over 400 miles away to the east, and from it I could glimpse the summits of other high points in the Grampians, over towards Torridon in the west, Lochnagar further east, Ben Lomond to the south, and beyond – each one rising above the blanket of cloud that lay far below my boots.

Many translate the name of Ben Nevis to mean 'Malicious Mountain'; others argue that the word Nevis comes in fact from the word 'neamh' which instead would make it 'Mountain of Heaven'. I confess I'd all too often experienced it with a personality more in common with the malicious interpretation, but in the conditions that morning, with the sun shining down above the clouds, giving me what felt like a summer's day while people in the valley below were likely having to put on an extra jumper and crank up the central heating, I felt like this really was paradise.

With such fantastic conditions I toyed with the idea of staying that night in the storm shelter. I paced over to it, climbing the steps made slick with a thin layer of ice, and removed the large metal latch to open the door. Jokes abound about this place, with its reputation for being the world's highest urinal legendary, but when I opened the door it wasn't that smell that greeted me, but one much, much worse.

The sweet stench of rotting rubbish gathered cloud-like as I pushed my body into the gap. Abandoned apple cores, bottles of whisky, beer, champagne and energy drinks, rotting half-eaten sandwiches and the ubiquitous toilet paper were strewn all over the floor. I felt disgusted and instantly sick.

I remembered reading somewhere how, back in 1819, a naturalist had come to the summit and been disappointed to find discarded pieces of glass, chicken bones, corks and bits of paper. It was sad that, in the nearly 200 years since his observation, we hadn't seemed to have got any better.

Inside the floor was wet, soaking through from the condensation created by a warmer space in below-freezing conditions. The wooden floor was buckling under it, and a Therm-a-Rest air mattress, left behind for others to use, was completely saturated, meaning sitting on it would be wetter than sitting on the floor. With the smell so overpowering I kept the door wide open, hoping the fresh air would dissipate the stench. I crawled inside and sat on the slightly raised platform and looked at the walls, the wood scratched by recent occupants wanting to mark their time here. I've never understood the human being's need to ruin a place in such a way; surely the memory here should be enough. There I sat for a minute, which became several, which became hours. I watched through the door as one by one people reached the trig point, took their photograph and left. From the group raising money for cancer, to a French fell runner who came up to say hello (I made him a coffee in return), the American couple from the hostel, and a couple of Polish boys. Each time one of them popped their head into the shelter I remarked on the rubbish, trying hard to impress upon them how bad it was.

I could have easily stayed there that night. I had enough supplies to keep me reasonably well fed, and enough water to make drinks, but that rubbish glared over to me, seemed to burn an impression into my soul. I set about collecting it in two plastic bags, one which I had brought with me for my own waste products, and the other that was itself discarded there. I collected it all into these two big bags and sat them in the corner wondering what I might do next. This had ruined everything.

It's not the first time (and sadly won't likely be the last) that rubbish on The Ben has been a cause for concern to someone. When the southern portion of the estate was bought by the John Muir Trust back in the year 2000, it became a hotly debated topic. In 2005 a man called Robin Kevan, aka 'Rob the Rubbish', came to the top to clean up the mountain. Then the following year a decision was made to remove the huge numbers of memorial plaques that people had thought to place on top of the summit.

Now, nearly ten years later, it was my turn to set an example. If I stayed here continuing my challenge in these freezing conditions, the fog now coming and going thick and fast and plunging the mercury down to –5°C, I would be far too tired to carry it down myself. With not a single other visitor who had seen it offering to help, I did the only thing I could with a clear conscience. I decided to abandon both my challenges and take it off the summit.

The journey down was painful and hard, painful because of hauling the extra weight I could have done without carrying, and hard because I had once again not delivered true on my challenge. Putting the latter problem to one side for the moment, I concentrated on lugging the rubbish bags down. A couple of walkers commented as they passed me, saying how bad it was I had found so much litter, though neither offered to help carry the burden.

Once I'd cleared the plateau proper I left the swirling mist that had enveloped the top. I checked my phone for the time and to my astonishment realised I had not just a mobile phone signal at my disposal but 3G as well. I took to Twitter, posting a photograph of me and my rubbish loot with the simple phrase: 'If I can carry this much down, why can't people take their own litter out?'

Feeling better for venting my problem, I stopped a couple of steps later when my phone bleeped to signal a message. Someone had retweeted my post. I put the phone away and no sooner than I had it beeped again, and again and again and again. My tweet was fast becoming viral, over 900 retweets already, over 800 favourite tags, and a host of others vocalising their horror at so much rubbish being left on such a beautiful mountain.

I was overwhelmed and felt the upper part of my nose fizz, as it always does when I attempt to hold back tears. To know that many others were with me on this, to see that perhaps my actions might stop just one other person littering our landscapes, or might cause them pick up someone else's just because I had shown that I would, made me feel more pride than completing my Extreme Sleeps Challenge ever could.

I groaned and ached all the way down the Pony Track, swapping the arms that carried the bags, spurred on by the constant beeps from virtual supporters of my cause. This was becoming something of a personal challenge of its own. Every time I stopped to rest, my knees would tremble uncontrollably, the extra weight truly taking its toll. My biceps burned as the bottles bashed against my legs, and even then I continued on.

At Half Way Lochan I stopped to watch the sun set, the cloud inversion now literally at my feet, the orange glow of the sun sinking behind it. To think that those people in the valleys I had briefly envied the night before would now be complaining of an awful cloud-covered day experienced, when mine had been one of the best, at least from a weather point of view. Nature had rewarded me with a visual memory I will take with me until the day I die, and it seemed only fair to reward her by clearing her, for now, of this man-made waste.

By the time I reached the A82 and my car by the hostel, I was practically in tears with the pain. It had been the hardest descent I had ever attempted, both physically and emotionally. I had wanted to give up several times, my back aching, my thighs and arms on fire, but I'd made an unwitting commitment by posting it on Twitter and had needed to see it through to the end.

Once at the building I walked past to the bins and placed the two bags inside. I had done it. Not the challenge I had set for myself, but a far greater one instead, one that I hoped may change the future for other mountains.

At that particular moment I didn't know what would become of my wild camping challenge – either of them – but at that minute it didn't matter. For now, it seemed, The Ben would wait.

THREE:

EXTREME SLEEPS CHALLENGE

CHAPTER SEVEN

CORRACHADH MÒR

Wind screeched all around me as I fought to climb over the fence. Over my shoulder I caught the flash from the lighthouse beam, making its endless circle in the dark. Water sprayed in my face, though I couldn't be certain whether it was spray from the sea or rain from the sky. I tightened the drawstrings around my hood, scrunching the fabric tightly to keep me warm inside. I knew this wasn't a long walk in terms of distance, but in these conditions I felt like I would never reach my destination.

Soon a river blocked my path, wide and fast flowing. Instantly I was transported back to Glencoul, the grip of the icy water bound like a corset around my lungs and my inability to breathe that day. I found myself backing away involuntarily. I headed upstream and to my relief found that it became narrow enough to jump across in one motion. I closed my eyes, took a deep breath and ran, leaping into the night, waiting to feel land beneath my feet once more...

After my unexpected litter-picking heroics on Ben Nevis I did wonder if I should abandon my Extreme Sleeps Challenge entirely – especially given that I had in essence already abandoned my attempt to complete my 3 Peaks Sleeps. After throwing away the rubbish at the hostel in Glen Nevis I had sat for several minutes in the darkened confines of my car, watching as the light from my door faded out. It was already dark again and my first sleep had been a complete disaster, with no summit claimed for the 6 hours I had set as the target. Following several minutes of silent contemplation I remembered that no good decision has ever been made on an empty stomach, and so I set off for Fort William and a good dose of chips.

As I began to feel my energy stores being replenished, the colour in my cheeks return and the blisters on my feet begin to throb, I decided that I should at least attempt to continue with my planned sleeps – the westernmost, easternmost, most northerly, most southerly, most central, highest and lowest points on mainland Britain, even if this first one had been a bit of a non-starter. I pulled out my road atlas and looked at my watch. Getting to Dunnet Head – the most northerly point – would take too long, the series of single-track roads likely overrun with deer now that night had fallen, which would make for not only a long, but also a dangerous route. Instead I looked to the westernmost point I'd identified, a hillock on the Ardnamurchan Peninsula in western Scotland.

Standing at around 36 metres above the waves, the stripy black-and-white lighthouse at Ardnamurchan Point is often mistakenly attributed as the most westerly point of mainland Britain. But it's not. In fact, the place that holds that honour is marked on the hillock of Corrachadh Mòr, where a small unassuming collection of rocks is placed to signify its position.

It only sits around half a mile south of the lighthouse, and from the road it doesn't actually look like it juts out into the sea any further than the lighthouse does, but my map told me otherwise and so I was on a mission to find it and sleep there. It looked quite far from Fort William, but a quick spot of Googling soon revealed that I could be over onto the right spit of land if I caught the last car ferry over Loch Linnhe, just 40 minutes' drive from where I now sat off the A82 if I were to rush.

I gulped down the rest of my chips, followed by a big slurp of the last of my tea and ran for the car, the hailstones starting to fall as I did so. I looked back up the valley towards the summit of Ben Nevis before I left, the whole bulk of hills now lost to the storm clouds. I was pleased I wasn't on the top of the mountain now – I would be freezing in the refrigerator-like survival shelter in this weather.

I raced down the road fast, swearing at the drivers who were meandering along at 10 mph below the speed limit. It was painfully frustrating. I had gone from 'girl without a plan' one minute to 'woman on a mission' the next and it seemed like everything was conspiring against me.

Finally I reached the ferry turn-off and saw the ship waiting, half loaded. I swerved down to reach it, for a minute panicking that I didn't have any cash, then remembering the emergency £20 I kept stashed in my first aid kit.

The ferry hand gestured for me to move forward and slowly I crept up onto the boat. The rain was still pelting down mercilessly and inside the warmth of my car the glass began to steam up with condensation. I reluctantly wound down the window.

'Did I need to buy a ticket before I boarded or can I just pay you?' I asked the ferry hand urgently as he directed me into a space.

'Well, you can pay me if you like, love, but I will just pocket the cash!' came the reply. 'Best wait till the ticket guy comes to you, I reckon.'

I thanked him and rolled up the window, rifling around for my note. Soon I had paid and we were off, the water flat calm beneath the ferry, the rain a torrent above it. My windscreen wipers were on full and still it was difficult to make out what was outside. I looked to Google maps on my phone to work out which way I needed to turn when I got off. It appeared that once I came off the ferry, as long as I turned left then kept straight for a good while, ignoring any turn-offs, I would soon be nearing my planned sleep.

A slamming grind of metal on concrete alerted me to the fact that we had arrived and I dutifully followed the two cars ahead of me off. We set out as a trio, sticking together for the first few metres, but then one turned off almost immediately, heading home to a warm bed. But not me. The other turned off soon after, likely also heading home given that it was now getting close to 9 p.m. Still I continued along the road. Soon the headlights from the car behind disappeared into the darkness. I was alone.

Looking at the GPS map on my phone I knew I was somewhere close to the edge of the water, skimming it to my left. Somewhere below me there was a drop and so I edged my way along slowly, knowing that as long as I got there before midnight all would be well.

Ardnamurchan can be reached without using the ferry I had taken. A single-track road leads along its southern and northern edges, joining it up to the mainland road network further inland. But it's far easier and quicker to take the ferry. Due to its remoteness this 130-km-square peninsula is renowned for having the largest concentration of Gaelic speakers in the whole of Scotland – I guess where people are cut off from the mainland, the more likely it is that older traditions will survive.

Indeed, it is a place that I had wanted to visit for years but it had always seemed too far out of the way to bother with and so I had relegated it to my 'one-day list', with other better places to see taking priority in the meantime. Now I was exploring it by the light of my headlamps only, but I hoped very much that I would soon get to see it clearly by daylight and that it would reveal itself to be worthy of the journey.

I swung around another bend to see the water of the loch reflecting back at me. Soon after a tiny hamlet seemed to merge into the view, being only a small cluster of homesteads, each looking as warm and inviting as the hostel at Glen Nevis had the previous day. I made a note to return there the following morning to see if I could bag me a cooked breakfast before I headed north.

The road ahead once more seemed devoid of people and I had to focus hard to keep myself from falling asleep. I passed an imposing-looking hotel one minute, then sped by a small cart selling fruit the next, with an honesty box alongside it welcoming payment. Never mind leaving the main roads, I felt like I'd stepped back in time.

After seeing no one for what seemed like an age I rounded a corner to be faced with a whole gang of workmen repairing the road. They had on their bright halogen lights and for a moment it was as though it was daytime again. One of them gestured for me to stop; he looked as confused by my presence as I was by his. He came to my window. I was expecting to be confronted with the thick accent of a native Gaelic tongue, but instead, with a decidedly Polish intonation, came the request: 'Please wait for my signal to go.' It seemed we were both foreigners in this rugged landscape.

I think they were placing piping or cables and watched as a team of four fought to cover over the huge vein-like hole they had been digging so that I might find my way across it. They gestured for me to come and soon I left them and their fluorescent orange-and-yellow suits behind. I was back to the lonely road once more.

Shortly after, the eyes of a deer became caught in my headlights and I slowed to watch a doe mosey on across the tarmac in no particular hurry, eventually stepping down off it so that I could pass. Just before I did, a mouse took its chance and whizzed across too – there was certainly an abundance of life here on this oft-forgotten peninsula.

As I drove the rain seemed to become heavier still and once again I cursed myself for planning the expedition in November, the most changeable and unpredictable of months. If I'd had my way – and the foresight to plan better – I would have come here in the summer when wild-camping spots remained relatively dry and therefore usuable. At any point in time I knew that my whole challenge could be put on hold or called off completely – as indeed it had been the previous night when I'd been kept away from my summit goal. As the road became suddenly overhung by a canopy of old trees, my headlights seemed to glow brighter, but nothing looked appealing. I began to wish I was back on The Ben again.

I passed a couple of farms and a whole host of static caravans seemingly facing out to sea and the brunt of the wind. I thought back to the survival shelter on top of the mountain; surely these little tin boxes were no warmer or secure than that? Still I headed west.

Finally I saw a sign that I had been keeping my eyes peeled for the entire time: 'The Lighthouse'. I was nearly there. One more climb and an additional bend and I began to see the beam from the lighthouse rotating ahead. I was doing well for time, it now being a little before 11 p.m. I drove until the road ended at the base of the tower. There a number of cars waited outside and a sign advised that this was a no-parking zone. I drove back down away from it and on the other side of the bridge a lay-by looked a likely candidate, so I pulled in. Almost immediately afterwards, the lights from another car sped behind me, leaving the lighthouse and heading for the small village I had passed on my way in. The reflective orange of the word 'COASTGUARD' flashed in my rear-view mirror and I looked to see them hurtling along the road, eager to call it a night here and find comfort somewhere warm.

My car shook as the wind gusted beneath its wheel arches and threatened to pull it over. Not an ideal night for a tent sleep, but one I was now determined to do. Water splashed down on the windscreen and on the side windows, a mix of rain and seawater blown off course. The sound of the waves was an echoing roar, so loud that it seemed endless in its reverb.

I pulled on my jacket and got out of the car to check I was OK to leave the vehicle there. There seemed to be no signs like there were up by the lighthouse, then I spotted a wooden post that had been knocked down by the gusts. I picked it up, the white words staring me plain in the face: 'No Parking.' I turned it over and placed it back on the floor face down. I got into the car, the metal walls shaking violently in the gusts, and contemplated my next move.

What seemed like seconds later I was startled by yet another passing car. It was make or break time. I was either going to do this sleep or I wasn't. I looked to the back seat where my Go Bag sat packed and ready to go, and beside that my little camera, with which I was meant to be filming. I had run out of excuses. It was now or never. I lurched for my rucksack, unclipped my seatbelt and opened the car door. I had begun.

Almost immediately and with a smile slowly spreading on my face I realised that the conditions weren't quite as bad as the sound had implied inside my vehicle. Sure, it was windy and, yes, I was getting pummelled by gusts of rain and seawater, but this was doable. I switched on the camera and said a few words and noticed that already the battery was starting to wane.

I had no paper map to help me. I had neglected to pick one up at the services en route, so spur-of-the-moment had my rush to catch the final ferry been, but I had found the location on my Streetmap app while sitting on the ferry and I had taken a photograph of the relevant section of the OS map on my phone. The GPS on Google maps, although not connected to the internet, could still find me and between these two slightly unorthodox tools I felt confident I could achieve my goal.

I walked along the road a little first, noting that I would need to cross the fence to gain access to the land. On the drive down I hadn't noticed a stile or other helpful aid to get me across, but I knew that if I walked far enough I would find a weak spot where I could climb it and not do any damage to it. I could see from the cables that it was, rather unhelpfully, also an electric fence, and I felt a kind of mild panic rising in my tummy as I fought to work out whether or not it was on. A quick search in the undergrowth and I found a generator. This seemed to be connected to the fence. Perhaps in summer it runs constantly, as tourists descend on what they believe to be the westerly point and take a tour of the lighthouse. Now, in late November, heading fast towards December, the owner clearly figured it would be a waste of petrol and had not bothered to switch it on.

It was a chance I would have to take. I removed my glove and placed the back of my hand on it slowly. I braced myself for a twinge but, thankfully, none came. I braved to touch it again with my fingers and quickly realised my hunch had paid off. It was not connected; I was safe to pass.

Remembering my promise to the filmmaker I did a quick garbled bit to camera. I didn't mind having it with me, but keeping a video diary was already becoming a little tedious, as though I had to explain myself at every footing, something I rarely took the time to do anymore as I was used to walking and camping alone.

I climbed over the fence. A few steps later in the darkness I could make out the shape of two deer standing on top of the rise in front of me, my approach clearly disguised by the noise of the waves crashing and the howling wind. It was then that the wind picked up and I realised I needed to cross the first river. Battening down my hood and sleeves I made a run for it and leapt across the fast-flowing water, hoping I would make it in one jump.

I did – just. My right foot connected with the opposite bank while my left trailed slightly in the water, generating a splash.

I let out a triumphant yelp and startled the deer, watching as their white tails bobbed off into the distance, seemingly swallowed up in the swell.

The ground was boggy and wet beneath my feet and sucked at my ankles with force. Using the light from my head torch I picked my path forward as though skipping in an imaginary flagstone minefield, careful not to step on the cracks. The grassy tussocks held firm for me and soon I reached a little rise affording me a view back to the lighthouse, its bright beam illuminating my surrounds. Here the ground became solid under my feet. It was still grass, but rather than thickets of long straw-like reeds interspersed with puddles of mud, this was meadow-like, even and soft. I could hear it swish against my trousers as I paced forward. It took all my mental strength to not stop there, to not put down my bag and pitch up my tent, knowing that I was only off the most westerly point by less than a mere kilometre.

I may not be good at climbing, may lack the upper-body and leg strength required to make me a good cyclist or an ironman competitor, may have spent my schooldays getting an 'acceptable' for my level of fitness and a 'cause for concern' for my attitude towards exercise, but, despite all my athletic shortfalls, what I lack in agility I more than make up for in bloody-minded stubbornness and unfailing blind optimism.

And so, knowing that whatever was thrown at me I would and I could make it to my goal that night, I continued south where almost immediately I was faced with another river to cross. 'Bollocks!' I shouted loudly to the wind and stood as the word was carried away with it.

Once more too wide, and made too dangerous by a fast-flowing current, I looked to the ground for signs of where to go next. Guessing by the ray of my head torch I found and followed what appeared to be a sheep track, hoping at least that my four-legged counterparts would also have looked for the line of least resistance.

Luckily my woolly companions did not fail me. Soon the water narrowed to little more than an inlet that I could stride across without even the need for a long run-up. I smiled to myself – I was going to make this sleep.

Some more tussocks, bogs and wet socks later I came to the final obstacle, a wide body of water. This time, however, I could make out that it came in to some kind of natural bay; I thought I might even be able to spy sand. I headed inland and negotiated my way round some sheep that seemed unconcerned by my presence. Soon I passed what looked like proper man-made walls – the remains of a homestead I figured, though without a roof – and then I began to climb a gentle incline. My destination had to be around here somewhere. I pulled out my phone and looked at the photo of the map. I had crossed the right number of rivers and circumnavigated the bay; I was nearly there. I continued up and then switched Google maps back on. It located me as a friendly blue blob and the appearance of a pile of stones confirmed my position. I was there, the most westerly person on mainland Britain, and it was still before midnight. The challenge was on.

The origins of people on this fairly inaccessible peninsula can be traced back hundreds of years. Small communities seemed to live here as early as the 700s and records show battles taking place here at least as far back as that as well. Closer to the present day, the remains of a Viking burial ship found here have been moved for safe-keeping at the West Highland Museum in nearby Fort William. As recently as 2011, reports show that a tenth-century ship was found at nearby Eilean Mhòir, with a collection of goods that included a spear and a sheaf in keeping with the theory that the dead man who had possessed them was in fact an important warrior. Viking graves have also been found on the peninsula, with spoils that came from Norway and Ireland found inside.

As I erected my tent on the little high point just in front of the cairn, I imagined the sea full of ornate, wooden Viking ships being tossed on the frothing waves. The lighthouse beam now replaced the flame of a beacon that our ancestors would have erected to warn of land, the storm raging against it in an attempt to beat it out as soldiers battled to keep it alight. Who knows, maybe ancient families had huddled in the same spot I did now, seeking shelter from the elements.

I snuggled into my sleeping bag, still full from my dinner of chips earlier, feeling satisfied for once, having achieved the first true sleep on my Extreme Sleeps Challenge here on Britain's most westerly point. Lost to my dreams of warriors landing in storms, it wasn't long before sleep found me, and my 6-hour rule as a minimum sleep time was soon obeyed.

The most recent census put the population of the Ardnamurchan Peninsula at around 2,000, with most dwelling in villages with delightfully tongue-twisting names such as Acharacle, Achnaha, Ockle, Portuairk and Sanna, to name a few. That night, in the refuge of my tent on the small summit of Corrachadh Mòr, I managed to boost the population to around 2001.

I meant to leave early the following morning, as I always try to when I wild camp, just as the sun rises. At it happens, I didn't, and instead awoke to the glowing walls of my tent lighting my warm cocoon in pinkish rouge.

Whenever I wild camp and wake up in a location I have never before visited, I always savour what I call my 'reveal moment', the first time I open my tent flap and spy, often with a true sense of awe, the beautiful surrounds in which I have managed to make my bedroom for the night.

From the colour of my tent walls I could tell that I was in luck. I had woken up in some rather splendid weather conditions, my previous night's effort battling with wind making it all the more worthwhile. I began my ritual, adding a layer for warmth and sneaking out through my tent flap, slowly unzipping the outer zip and poking my head out into the unknown.

I savoured every second and gasped in wonder as I saw the lighthouse shining in a dawn sunlight, its white stripes turned almost amber in the early-morning light. I turned to look behind me, then remembered my camera. It was starting to feel like Wilson, the basketball in the Tom Hanks film *Castaway*. As though I had another person with me, who kept holding me back from doing what I really wanted to do. For a minute I resented it. I didn't want to share this special moment with anyone, and wondered why on earth I had offered to share it with people in the first place. Then I caught myself and remembered. I was trying to get others to fall for these wild places as hard as I had, so I needed to show them everything about it that was good, not just moan to camera when things were less than perfect.

And so I backtracked inside the tent and replayed my movements, admitting to anyone who might one day be watching that I had already taken a sneaky peek at what awaited outside. Despite it being my second go at it, I still gasped when I caught sight of the lighthouse, the land fringed like pieces of a jigsaw puzzle along the edge of the shore leading up to it. I stepped outside onto the carpet of grass at my feet and spun around to face the interior. This was genuinely the first time I had seen this landscape, too, and I could not hide my ecstasy at the jagged mountains that greeted me.

I had passed them all in the car at night, but had not had a chance to really appreciate the topography in any real way. Now they loomed like giant molars belonging to a mythical beast, the sunlight cracking and splitting into a thousand pieces as it rose over the top of them. Another mound of hulking rock rose up to my right. This part of the peninsula is what remains of a giant volcanic complex and the land folds and spreads as though lava was just spilling into the sea and cooling to form land. I'm no geologist and I'm sure one would correct me, but standing here now it looked as though it had frozen only very recently, trapped in time by the cooling effect of the Atlantic Ocean.

Across the waves, what I thought in the dark had been lamps on big sailing vessels actually turned out to be lighthouses and warning beacons on the opposite island of Mull. I stood and gawped at the scene for several minutes without moving, breaking my gaze with the surrounds only once to switch off the camera after noticing the battery life was getting seriously low. It was funny. This place was never one I had had on my radar as a priority to visit, having been hell-bent instead on seeking out a lot more of the high mountains and wild places Scotland has to offer, rather than a tiny hill on the western reaches of an unpronounceable peninsula. But my challenge had brought me to it, and it now rated as one of the best reveal moments of my wild-sleeping career.

Content, I set about making breakfast, congratulating myself on a good find and wondering what other treasures my challenge would yet afford me. A high-pitched whistle made me turn my attention back towards the interior, where I saw an abundance of sheep released near the bay I had passed in the dark – no shepherd could be seen.

I packed away my belongings quickly and scrambled onto the limpet-covered rocks to stare out at the waves. Having grown up near the sea, I find that the coast holds a truly special place in my heart. I can be easily hypnotised by the dance of the waves, staring for hours as they lull and crash together. I remember a cartoon I watched as a little girl called *The Last Unicorn*, where the remaining one of the species on land discovers (spoiler alert for anyone who hasn't yet seen it) that all the others still actually exist, but are now in the sea. Thousands upon thousands of them made up the frothing white horses, the tips of the waves that crashed upon the beach and raced up the land. I found it the most magical revelation at the tender age of six. And now, a great many years later, I still remember it, still watch for the unicorns whenever I find myself staring at the waves.

Even from my vantage point now, at the very last reaches of solid ground, which just last night were covered in briny seawater, I looked at the lighthouse and it seemed as though it was further west than me. But eyes are funny things, never to be believed. I know for a fact that this Scottish spot is further west than any other point of mainland Britain – beating the famous Land's End in Cornwall even by a good 20 miles. And a quick search on the internet will inform you that where I slept that night was at least 30 metres further west than the beautiful Ardnamurchan Point.

I headed back to the cairn that denotes the top of Corrachadh Mòr – whose name, I find out later, translates to 'tapering field' – and began to retrace my steps from the night before. At the little bay the sheep were munching busily on the kelp that had washed up to shore in the storm. I sat on the wall of a homestead that had once sat at the head of this bay. The more I stared about it, the more I could see that nature had carved here a very natural harbour, complete with ramp-like side rocks suitable for launching a boat.

Overhead a white-tailed eagle bounced on the thermals, its sharp claws visible despite its height over me. I took a moment to spin around a full 360 degrees – the views of coast, mountain, coast, mountain soared past my eyes, each one as perfect as the next. I wished I could stay here forever, rebuild this shack by the sea and get myself a boat to fish in the waters. I would keep sheep for the wool to manufacture my own clothing and learn how to cook seaweed in a way that it didn't taste merely of salt water – I would be like Margaret Elliot of Glencoul here on this peninsula. I set up my camera to take a video moment of this perfect bay, of me walking in the sand in this dappled sunlight, the sky cobalt blue and the waves merely lapping the shore. At which moment the battery died.

It was a sign that I had lingered too long. I had begun my Extreme Sleeps Challenge at last and, if I hurried, I would have time to make the next planned sleep in relative comfort.

I would soon discover that the small hamlet I had noted on the way in did not offer any establishments that served anything in the way of refreshments or breakfasts; for that I would have to wait until I left the peninsula proper. But for that one perfect moment I enjoyed my blissful residence, dreamed of a time that would never be and congratulated myself on a job well done.

I began to head back to the car, the north now fixated in my head, the second point in my plan to sleep Britain's extremes. Just then, the rain started falling; it was to be another wet night.

CHAPTER EIGHT

DUNNET HEAD

Take out a map of Scotland and look to its northernmost edge at the top-right corner of the mainland, just below the Orkney Islands. Jutting out into the sea you will find a hulk of a headland known as Dunnet Head. Along with the more famous point of John o'Groats 11 miles to the east, it forms the top of the bear's head that is seemingly trying to break away from the rest of Scotland. Dunnet Head – and more specifically the smaller Easter Head at its tip – is at the top of the bear's ear. It's here at this unassuming landmark, away from the tartan-themed souvenirs and sticks of rock of John o'Groats, that the true northerly point of the British mainland is found. This was to be the second in my Extreme Sleeps Challenge.

When I left Ardnamurchan I had plenty of time to kill before it was time to head for bed again – despite the long drive north – and so I decided to spend some time visiting the place most people assume to be the most northerly point in Britain first. The drive was a convoluted one, a steady meandering across the width of Scotland until I reached the east coast and then took a left turn tracing the coast north.

The rain that had started by the bay at Ardnamurchan in the west didn't leave me all that day; it still followed me now as I made my way up the east coast. Between the towns were sea views, some close to the car window, others locked away by drives down small roads. I stopped a couple of times to take a peak, and detoured once through a very out-of-place-looking housing estate with large white homesteads, where a winding road took me down to the sea. Crab nets lay bundled and the cafe, which a series of signs had assured me would be waiting at the bottom, complete with a bevy of hot drinks, toilets and Scottish hospitality, turned out in fact to be closed for the season.

Instead I sat outside it, hungry. In my frustration I nibbled on an oatcake that I found in my glove compartment – a thoroughly unsatisfying snack. Despite it being November, I reasoned that my best bet for a bite to eat of something more substantial would be found in the tourist trap that masquerades as the northernmost point of the British mainland.

I put my foot down and headed to a place I never thought I'd be particularly bothered about seeing. Before the end point itself, while driving along what appears to be just an open expanse of countryside, the roadside sign announcing John o'Groats suddenly makes an appearance, welcoming you to 'The end of the road'.

I continued on past the sign, splashing through standing road water as I did so.

I don't know quite what I expected to be at the end of the road – a sign perhaps, one of those comedy crossroad markers seen on places all over the world telling you how many miles you are from places like New York, Tokyo and Sydney. What actually appeared there was a car park, and this one clearly meant business. With spaces for tens of coaches and hundreds of cars, I did for one minute wonder if that was, in fact, all that John o'Groats offered visitors – a giant car park.

With only a handful of other people there, I drove past the empty spaces to get as close as I could to the buildings. There was a cluster of what seemed to be identical souvenir shops, selling everything a visitor to this faux landmark could possibly want – from T-shirts to tea towels, it seemed that anyone who made the pilgrimage to this great place would want to memorialise the occasion on some piece of tat. As exclusively forecast, there was also a comedy crossroad marker to have your photograph taken at.

There was an impressive-looking, modern cafe with picture-window views out over Stroma and beyond to the Orkney Islands, but I guffawed when I saw the price of crisps was well over a pound – I dared not ask the price of a sandwich – and so I left more or less as quickly as I had arrived, determined to buy myself a more reasonably priced meal a bit further along the 'end of the road'.

I could have lingered a little, booked myself a ticket on the ferry that sets course not far from there for the Orkney Islands, but of course I didn't, not wanting to risk missing out on my next successive sleep on one of the British mainland's true extremities.

'The end of the road' is a misleading name, of course, because the main road doesn't actually end at John o'Groats; you just have to make a left turn at the appropriate place and head instead to Thurso. For the next 20 minutes, driving west from John o'Groats, the small towns passed on the way might lull you into a false sense of security that you have indeed escaped the masses. You haven't. Thurso is a town that, in the scheme of things up here, is quite large in stature. Positioned around a naturally shaped bay it offers a collection of houses, cafes and small shops perfect for mooching around.

I stayed in one such establishment, drinking multiple cups of tea and feasting on a more reasonably priced sandwich and packets of crisps, until I spied the colours of sunset at the window. I waited until the sky turned orange, then, despite the heavy rain, I got back on the road and set a course for the headland at Dunnet Head, the true northerly point of mainland Britain.

I don't know why it irks me so much that people think it's John o'Groats, and even more so when people attempt to cover the length of Britain by going from it to Land's End, rather then travelling from Dunnet Head to Lizard Point. I mentally make a note to myself that I should invent a new challenge after this one that does just that, before dismissing the idea immediately when I remembered that I too am doing an equally random challenge for no particular reason I can fully explain.

Like most of these promontories – I was fast discovering – no one seemed to care about them representing the real extremes of the British mainland apart from me. There was no sign directing people to Corrachadh Mòr so that they may stand at the most westerly point and, as I drove up the single-track road towards the headland limit of the Pentland Firth, there was no 'Did you know' kind of sign informing me that I was indeed heading to the true north of the mainland.

To reach it I took the B855 road from Brough up to the tiny village of Dunnet – which is, in case you were wondering, also the northernmost road on mainland Britain. Such is the shape of the headland here, stretching as it does both north and west into the rough seas of the Atlantic, that the similarly named Dunnet Bay nearby (which boasts one of the best Camping and Caravan Club sites that exists in the country, in my humble opinion) is sheltered from the worst of the typically bad ocean weather.

The road round to it from Dunnet bends and swerves over some very barren-looking land devoid of any real signs of life. The houses before the turn-off seemed full of character, with windmills and gnomes in the gardens, the personal touches of those within, but the drive on to Dunnet is not blessed with any type of uniqueness. It seemed to lack any kind of memorable features.

I continued along the road, slightly perturbed by the regular appearance of 'No overnight stopping' signs, considering Scotland is supposed to be the best part of the UK for wild camping, and, at length, finally arrived in the public car park – I was the only one there. I stopped just next to the slate sign that understatedly says 'Dunnet Head: Most Northerly Point of Mainland Britain. Welcome.' Behind it an interpretation board advises of some of the birds you might see and a small, squat, white lighthouse sits beyond, its light illuminating the grey fog with a fuzzy yellow glow.

Though a little underwhelmed, I was now in 'challenge mode' and took a look at the map to work out where best to leave the car. I figured that leaving it as the only one there next to the lighthouse would attract too much attention, particularly as it appeared that a couple of employees were inside the lighthouse, and given the proliferation of 'No overnighting' signs I had passed on the way in.

Looking at the OS map I could see that there was something of a high point a couple of hundred metres from where I was, at around 127 metre spot height, and a rough but perfectly accessible road to take me there. I crept the car along it and, arriving (to my delight) with military precision at the exact high point, I left my vehicle at a wide spot just a little after its terminus, beneath something of a tiny summit.

My reference to the military was not far off the mark. Back in 1939, in the midst of the understandable paranoia of war, a number of radar stations were set up around the British coastline to check for U-boats that might be passing by. Dunnet Head was the site for such a one, the powers that be worried that these enemy submarines might utilise the Fair Isle Channel to manoeuvre to and from the Atlantic Ocean. Operated by the Royal Navy, a series of six stations were erected, the one at Dunnet Head on the mainland and another five dotted around the islands to the north: two at Fair Isle, one at South Ronaldsay, one at Saxa Vord and one at Sumburgh. Known as the Admiralty Experimental Stations, the one at Dunnet Head was the last to be built, with the structure completed in 1940 and positioned just near to where I had parked my car. As a Coast Defence U-boat Radar Station, it was designed to offer a first line of coastal defence, forming part of an early-warning network around the UK.

According to historical records, these radars were very efficient, able to detect and pinpoint the locations of ships and submarines to an accuracy of a couple of miles – the technology also allowed the Royal Navy to pick up any aircraft within a range of 100 miles.

I made my way now across the muddy ground, just able to make out the shapes of the ruined buildings that surrounded this important base 75 years ago. Now little more than the foundations or shells of their former structures remain, rising shapes in this rainy night. At the time two huts were built to house the transmitter and receiver respectively, the aerials positioned on top with the help of a series of scaffold structures. Tuned by hand only, they were operated by the staff who manned them from their time of completion in December 1940.

Operations continued over the next three years, with continual improvements in line with new technological advances. By 1942 only one aerial was required. At the end of 1943 the Royal Air Force took over operation until the station closed at the end of the war.

Now a sorry collection of ramshackle concrete huts, it was hard to believe the important role that these buildings had once played in the war effort. I found it strange that many of the locations I had visited so far – with the exception of the westernmost point, which had seen battle of a much different kind at the time of the Viking invasion – had played a pivotal role in the Second World War.

I continued on past these war relics and downhill back towards the car park I had left not long before, my feet becoming wet as I sploshed through puddles that were vibrating as raindrops splashed into them. Dressed in my darkest hill gear, I felt as though I was on some king of reconnaissance missions to seek the truest northerly point.

I walked through the car park almost on tiptoes and noticed happily that there was now only one car left in the private car park of the lighthouse. It was only a little past 9 p.m. and, eager to escape the rain, I went back to the warmth of the car, repacked my bag and waited for the moment to claim my wild sleep.

The wind whistled loudly, as it usually does in higher, end-of-the-world places like this, but the rain had begun to thin. As wild camping is not particularly encouraged there, I decided I would ready myself entirely for sleep before I left the car. My video camera was out of juice so I didn't have to worry that the tiny light from it might give me away in the dark. I could rest assured that I would go unseen. I wouldn't take a stove, so that the flame from that couldn't give me away either.

The lighthouse spun around methodically as I sat there passing the time. On paper, the adventure of sleeping at the extremes of Britain had looked rammed full of excitement, and it is true that I was often forced to battle with time and bad weather against me. Yet here, with a road that reached to within less than kilometre of the point I needed, it had seemed too easy.

After eating virtually every food supply I could find, listening to music on my iPhone until it too gave up the ghost, and becoming tired of rewiping my body-heat-produced condensation from the windscreen for the umpteenth time, I decided that enough was enough. I would head out there, a little past 11 p.m. by now, and wake up around 6 a.m., just before the sun rose, thereby fulfilling my self-imposed 6-hour rule and curtailing the risk of someone spotting me and giving me a good old-fashioned dressing down.

I bundled an extra jacket into the bag and headed out, wincing as I pushed the button to lock the car, because its lights suddenly illuminated the darkness more brightly than the lighthouse beam had managed to. The rain had stopped, though a dampness lingered in the air. I retraced my steps over the old army buildings, ignoring my eyes' determination to find human-being shapes among their structures, strode past the car park limits and made my way, cautiously, to the land's edge.

I could hear it way before I reached the lip of the cliff, the incessant crescendo of the waves crashing against land. Before I had come here I had wondered if I should try somehow to make my way instead down to the beach and out onto the rocks beneath the headland. But November high tides and my inability to fully understand them with any confidence had seen me rethink that plan. It would be something of a rude awakening to find myself bobbing out to sea on my sleeping mat in lilo-like fashion.

I made my way past the lighthouse building's boundaries, kneeling down to watch the windows for any signs of life. With none of them illuminated and no movement as far as I could tell, I snuck around to the ground in front of the lighthouse and unrolled my bivvy bag. Kicking off my boots was the most stressful bit, as I was upright, shaped like a person attempting to do a rather risky sleep near some cliff edges. My socks were immediately wet and I moved quickly to get inside my bivvy. Not wanting to take any chances – I am quite a mobile sleeper, often accused of 'sausage-rolling' the duvet – I had brought with me two sturdy, steel tent pegs and with them I secured my bivvy bag into the ground either side of me, to prevent myself from rolling off down into the crashing waves below.

Secure, I snuggled inside my bed and hoped to sleep as well as I had the previous night. Instead, I found myself wide awake. I could smell the ground, wet and earthy, but unlike the time I had escaped the perils of the water at Glencoul and been glad of its reassuring, life-affirming scent, it now just made me feel a little miserable. Made cold by the wind being brought inland from the sea, and without a good walk in to render me too tired to care, I lay awake, counting the minutes. I tried to imagine the views that I might awake to, perhaps over to the Old Man of Hoy on the Orkneys to the north, or out towards the island of Stroma to the east, but instead all I did was become increasingly distracted by the great circling beam of light on its endless cycle above my head. This was not a sleep I was hoping to repeat again any time soon.

I resolutely closed my eyes and found myself thinking back instead to the remains of the radar station and bunkers that lay a few hundred metres to the south beyond the lighthouse. I imagined myself here now, late at night, not trying to sleep but instead fighting the urge to nod off, charged with watching the radar for enemy ships or fighter jets. I pictured this jutting-out piece of mainland alive with the buzz of alert soldiers. I had learned that the military were again stationed here during the Cold War, the nights filled with the beep of radar, the days filled with gunfire, as the troops trained on the now defunct artillery range, waiting for the 5-minute warning that never came.

Perhaps that explains, I mused, the location of the gunmaker's business that I spotted back on the A836 in the village, a place that not only manufactures firearms for hunters but also – I later read – authorises fishing permits to those hoping to catch one of the brown trouts stocked in the lochs around Dunnet Head.

Somewhere between guns and fish I must have dozed off, for when I next woke up light was beginning to break. I pulled out my watch to see that it was close to 6 a.m. I had not just met, I had exceeded my 6-hour rule. My sleep at the most northerly point of Britain was over, without any kind of drama or concerns.

Despite my plans I lay there for a while, in the dampness of a condensation-covered bivvy bag, staring up at the lighthouse that rose a fairly short 20 metres above my head. I remembered learning somewhere that it was built back in 1831 by famed lighthouse builder Robert Stevenson, himself the grandfather of the author Robert Louis Stevenson, who penned classics like *Dr Jekyll and Mr Hyde*. My sleep here, though restless at first, had been more Dr Jekyll than Mr Hyde, but I imagine it isn't always as tame.

I squeezed my way out of my sleeping bag, the down inside it matted slightly at the feet, and bundled it up quickly into my rucksack, nearly ripping the bivvy as I forgot about the tent pegs. I shook off the bivvy to try and remove the film of water that covered it, made wet from my own body heat and the early-morning dew. Rolling it up drenched my arms and my hands and I began to wish I'd had brought a towel with me. Over the wall I could see movement in the private car park and moved quickly back behind it lest I be seen. Not that anyone could do anything about it now, of course. I waited for a few minutes, cold despite my layers. I heard voices shouting over the wind and felt a pang of hunger hit my stomach, making it growl noisily.

I looked out to sea, temporarily rooted to the spot, not wanting to draw any attention to myself. The views were not forthcoming. Instead a squally collection of grey clouds were bounding towards the land – towards me. I couldn't fight it any more. Slinging the straps over my shoulders I would merely look like a walker out for an early stroll.

I felt the eyes of the men burn into me as I made my determined way towards the boundary wall and across it. I walked purposefully and without hesitation, knowing that if I made the mistake of locking gazes with either one of them I might be forced to explain myself.

Soon I was back at the car park, and with relief I was still walking by myself. Either my observers assumed I was just a hiker who had got slightly off trail or knew what I had been up to and didn't care. Either way, I was home free and bounded up the summit and over to my car. I piled in and, without stopping for a second look or even a photo, I hit the road – the true 'end of the road', heading south, the only direction I could go.

As I passed the northern reaches of Brough I noticed that there was actually a tourist information centre for Dunnet Head just off the B855, although from the looks of it a lack of interest had forced it to close down. I drove on by, partially saddened that the northernmost point no longer held any excitement for visitors and partially pleased that it didn't, leaving it crowd-free for what had been an easy night's sleep.

A little afterwards I passed a tourist coach bound for John o'Groats, taking another busload of people to buy sticks of rock and have their photo taken at the 'end of the road'. I smiled, and pointedly headed south, now bound for the centre of the world...

CHAPTER NINE

WHITENDALE HANGING STONES

'Go back! Go back!' came the call from somewhere in the murk. The air was so wet with moisture that I could feel strands of my hair dripping with newly formed droplets, running off down my neck, chilling my skin. The culprit responsible for the warning emerged from the long grass, his red hair distinctive in my torchlight. He was squat in build, but held his head high. He looked me in the eye and flinched a little, then puffed up his chest. 'Go back!' came a further call, but this time it came from over his shoulder. Grouse. I watched as a second grouse emerged from the tussocks. The two of them looked at each other for a minute and then back at me. I walked towards them and kept watching as a group of about five grouse now, including these two, launched into the air, giving away their camouflaged location in a single spreading of the wings. From somewhere much further away still another grouse cry came, a throated and distinct call that always sounds as though they are warning you to 'Go back'.

They are a staple sight in the Forest of Bowland, a great trough of sweeping peat moorland, in hues of russet, amber and barley, that spread out on the high gritstone terrain and stretch down into yawning valleys in the heart of north-east Lancashire, where my challenge had brought me next. I'd never been here when it had not been raining – or at least when it had not been damp. Rain, it seems, makes little difference to the conditions here; whether sunny or stormy, the atmosphere is always dank and wet, so thick with melancholy it's as though you can cut it with a knife.

Ask any walker about the Forest of Bowland, particularly any walker who tried to hike here pre-2000, and they will likely regale you with tales of gamekeepers with guns warning you to 'Go back' in a much less friendly way than their feathered, resident counterparts. The land itself belongs to the Duchy of Lancaster aka HRH the Queen (so locals actually pay tax to Her Majesty) and it is looked after by an appointed Lord of Bowland. The main income here is not tourism, as with many other villages that stud some of the wilder places of England, Wales and Scotland, but actually shooting. The reason for the word 'Forest' in the name is because it was originally a 'royal hunting ground' and back in the day, in addition to grouse and the occasional deer, the likes of wild boar and even wolves would have been fair game to those with enough pennies to pay to shoot them.

Its lack of tourists makes it a truly unspoilt and pristinely inhospitable section of wilderness, which can catch even the most experienced unaware. Its lack of helpful signage is legendary. After driving nearly 450 miles from Dunnet Head to reach it – for it housed the third location in my Extreme Sleeps Challenge, the centremost point on mainland Britain – it was already 8 p.m. when I arrived.

I set out from the village of Dunsop Bridge on another rainy evening, guided only by the light of the moon. Shortly after leaving the small car park, I had already passed a sign advising that I was wandering on a private road and another 'Private' sign was nailed to the tree in a small thicket of woodland by the side of it. I was definitely in Bowland all right.

My hood rattled as the trees shook in the breeze and deposited a spray of raindrops over my head. I crossed a cattle bridge and could make out on either side of the gravel track I was on – stretching out straight to the cluster of terraced houses beyond – stacks of forested tree trunks lying in three separate bundles. I could make out some kind of a sign resting on the middle cluster. I wandered over for a closer look, half expecting to see some kind of 'Private' sign adorning them.

It was much worse. There, in frantically scrawled white paint, were the words: 'Do NOT play on the wood.' Yep, old habits die hard in the heartland of Bowland. With so many 'no' rules seemingly governing this part of England, I had been less than keen to come here. I'd been just three times before – not to the exact spot I was heading to now – but near enough to it to know what was in store. Each time the weather had been bad, or, maybe a fairer way of putting it, each time the weather had been typically Bowland in character. And every time the signs warning me to not go here or there had been rammed down my throat with such frequency that on each visit I had vowed not to bother returning again.

So it was with a heavy heart that I came back to Bowland on my challenge, especially given that my challenge involved me not only walking on land that people would like to stop me walking on, but also sleeping on that same forbidden land.

Deciding on the centre of Britain had certainly not been an easy task down the years, in fact no one seems to really agree on it at all – with several towns and villages laying claim to the title. One of the fiercest arguments is put forward by the town of Haltwhistle in Northumberland. It ubiquitously announces its claim to the accolade on fancy red banners and several shop signs. I remember seeing an article on the BBC in 2002 where one resident, who ran three such businesses that touted the centremost claim to fame, said that he, as an 'amateur cartographer', knew that Haltwhistle was the centre, because in a series of six different mathematical techniques he'd employed it was named to be so in 'most' of the cases. The fact that even he couldn't get all six to agree perhaps says a lot.

It's biggest rival, and the one that is officially named 'centre of Britain' by the mapping bigwigs at Ordnance Survey, is the one that I was heading for now, outside the village of Dunsop Bridge in Lancashire, about 71 miles south of Haltwhistle. How could it be so wildly far from Haltwhistle, I hear you ask? Well, the OS use what's known in mapping circles as the 'centre of gravity method'. For all those non-amateur cartographer enthusiasts, that basically means that they worked out the point at which they would need to place a drawing pin in a cardboard cut-out of Britain and make it still stay upright on a board.

Though described as the more official and technical of methods, it sounded rather *Blue Peter* and homemade to me

– the idea that any one of us could make such a stencil and attempt to underpin it somewhere to see if we could make it stand upright was so absurdly simple – at least compared with one accepted alternative of working out centroids and ellipsoids and calculating meridian lines and doing something involving projections.

Yep – give me a drawing pin and some paper and scissors and I will chose that option any day. And so it was with the OS method accepted that I started out from Dunsop Bridge, ignoring all the counter-arguments about whether or not you should include certain remote offshore islands in the calculation, and blindly shirking off the concept of shifting centre-points caused by erosion. Besides, if I had given those any heed, I would either be spending my night in the centre of a Northumberland town (which would have been a little tricky), or (perhaps worse) bedding down in a field just south of an NHS Mental Health Trust hospital near Whalley in Lancashire (considered to be the centremost point if not including any other islands save for the mainland of Great Britain).

Besides, BT had placed their bets on the Forest of Bowland by inserting their 100,000th payphone box there in 1992 with a notice that said: 'You are calling from the BT payphone that marks the centre of Great Britain.' Who was I to argue with BT?

I had approached the little town of Dunsop Head on a dark and rainy evening. I don't know what I really expected to greet me. There were no banners certainly. And no marker stones either. Nothing to give any indication that the centremost point of Britain was nearby. But I'll let you in on a secret. It isn't actually in this little hamlet that the centre-point sits anyway – this is merely the access point from which to reach it.

The true geographic centre resides around 7 kilometres further north than the village, at precisely the grid reference SD64188 56541 or, for those like me who need a more visual clue, at Whitendale Hanging Stones, which sit high on some rather bleak and boggy moorland above the last homestead at Brennand Farm.

I passed by the first of the houses down the track a little from the wooden trunks that were not for playing on. Soon after, I reached a gate that had attached to it (I only spied this thanks to the beam from one of the security lights of the houses) a little sign boasting of its accessibility to those who used mobility scooters.

A bit of an oxymoron in the Forest of Bowland – celebrating access. Until the Countryside Rights of Way Act (or CRoWA) came into being 15 years ago, most of the land I was walking on now would have been out of bounds. Unlike in Scotland, where everyone has the Right to Roam unless there is a good reason to prevent them, the law in England and Wales works in quite the opposite way. In those two countries it is assumed that you are walking on private land with no access rights, unless they have been specifically designated as rights of way. It is a thoroughly backwards way of looking at things in my opinion, and no doubt one of the reasons that headlines regularly carry stories of how children are exploring outside less and less.

There have always been people who think the way I do, perhaps most famously the people who worked in the industrialised cities of Sheffield and Manchester, who, sick of gazing longingly over to the wild and high places of the Peak District away from their urban sprawl, arranged a mass trespass over the hills to demand that they be granted the very basic right to go walking in the countryside. That was back in the 1930s and it made a huge impact in the struggle to guarantee that rights of way were opened up and that land was made accessible to the general public. That mass trespass was, albeit many years later, instrumental to the eventual success of the passing of the CRoWA which saw, for the first time in England and Wales, landowners having to justify why people couldn't walk on their land.

The famously closed-off swathes of the Forest of Bowland, locked away to walkers for decades if not centuries beforehand, suddenly looked like they might be opened up. It didn't happen overnight, of course. It took approximately five years for the legislative impact of the Act to be felt. Stiles were eventually erected, kissing gates installed and new Ordnance Survey maps released, showing for the first time huge palettes of yellow demarking access land for walkers.

In the Forest of Bowland it was cause for real celebration, as one by one the shouty 'Keep Out' signs that even lined the road along what's known as the Trough of Bowland began to come down.

Now I meandered up such a space, tracing the river as it cut along to my right, towards the dark and misty hills ahead. Despite the damp, it wasn't a particularly cold night – certainly not for the time of year. I passed another row of houses, noting how odd it was that in such spaces acres are left empty except for a sudden cluster of four homes all banded together tightly, each one overlooking the other.

The path began to fork, but a quick check of the map had me staying straight on. I was so close to houses that, despite my perfectly legal right to be there, I refrained from using my head torch as much as possible.

Shortly after, at the wall line, I spotted what appeared to be a large sign. Squelching over the muddy ground to get there, it making audible slurps as I went, I tried to read it. 'CAUTION,' it began, 'Nesting birds.' Then it continued on with a polemic about the risks of heading into 'Open Access' land and how you must obey a strict set of rules to protect the precious birds that lay their eggs in them. I snorted in retort.

When it comes to CRoWA, of course, there are exceptions. If a landowner has good reason to restrict access then they are allowed to – if they apply for specific permission. By far the most popular place in the country where this happens is the Forest of Bowland, where landowners are quick to cite interest in the protection of birds in their landscape. Don't get me wrong, I'm all about protecting birds too, and this particular area for one is home to the hen harrier, not to mention a host of other winged species. But what gets me is that many landowners don't want to protect them because they love birds, they want to protect them to look after their own assets – as it always was here in the 'royal hunting' ground, their main income remains from rich individuals who want to come and pay a lot of money to sit with a gun in a box, send a beater out ahead to scare the grouse into flight (very sportsmanlike) and them obliterate them with their rifles.

I continued on my path. Before the waterworks came a little barn, enclosed on all sides but one. With the rain picking up, I headed inside it and for the first time let my head torch go on to full beam. There was a little wooded bench behind me so I sat on it and took out a chocolatey snack, added an extra layer of clothing and opened up my map.

Going by the exact grid reference would take me to an unspecified lump of bog, so I was going to aim for the landmark beside it, the Whitendale Hanging Stones – which the OS people, after all, say is the centre. As I left my temporary shelter I saw yet another sign, this time advising that there was no camping allowed. I wilfully disobeyed it and walked past it with a big smirk plastered on my face.

As the road bent round to my left I could easily have followed it above the farm, but instead I spotted a fainter path leading up and across the flanks of the hill. I would rather be away from buildings and homestead tonight – away from people with difficult questions about why I was there in such weather and so late.

Despite the darkness the path was easy to find at first, the only levelled ground on the slope. I splashed through the puddles that had gathered in muddy pools, looking for firmer tussocks on which to plant my feet. Suddenly my nose filled with the smell of livestock, the sweet, sickly scent of manure, pungent and sharp despite the spits of rain. I did all I could not to breathe in too deeply.

When I came to the first gate on what was a public right of way, I found that the stile was blocked by a piece of fallen concrete, a sharp and rusty piece of metal rod protruding from it dangerously. The step up to the stile was snapped and broken, not weathered by age. Perhaps a relic from the earlier, less walker-friendly days.

Here the path went cold in the dark, the field ahead one rounded bump. I turned on my head torch briefly and found the tyre marks of 4x4s and quad bikes leading into the distance. I turned out the light once more. Lumps of sheep pellets lined the route around my feet, a kind of Hansel and Gretel breadcrumb trail leading me onwards. Every now and then my path would seemingly be blocked by a large, white boulder. I would switch on my light beam and then be confronted by a pair of eyes, made emerald in the torchlight, and the woolly boulder would move on by. Flies still circulated around the sheep and around my head and I fought to beat them aside as I continued on to a wall. The path had been churned up by excessive vehicle use and every so often stacks of soil blocked the route ahead and innocent-looking puddles revealed themselves to be ditches.

Finally I left this field and now needed to look for a wall over to my right, to use as a navigational handrail. Stopping me finding it immediately was a huge pile of farm spoil, blocking the natural route. It looked like getting to the centre-point of Britain was going to take some determination and willpower.

CLUNK! CLUNK! I heard the metal of some kind of tank or leftover animal feed bang as some sheep moved out of my way and brushed past it. As soon as I cleared the towering man-made hill of dirt I cut to my right. The ground was shaking under my boots; each step consisted of a slurp-suck-splat rhythm that would become my soundtrack.

I lost my footing to knee-deep water a couple of times, becoming swallowed up by the black ground at my boots; I was glad for my walking poles. A few years ago, in 2011, a very experienced fell runner called Bill Smith met his end in a peat bog here in the Forest of Bowland. Not unskilled in this environment, at the age of 75-years-young, he held a number of records and had once climbed no less than 63 Lake District peaks within a 24-hour time limit (a record beaten only by the legendary fell runner Joss Naylor). He also penned a book called *Studmarks on the Summits*, which is held in the highest reverence among followers of the sport. One fateful day he took the train from Ormskirk to Preston and, with a return ticket in his pocket, he headed up to the Trough of Bowland for a run. Somewhere around Saddle Fell he is thought to have fallen into the ice-cold waters of a peat bog where, unable to get out, and far from any help, he sadly perished. Well loved by all who ran with him, and at races where he acted as a marshal, he was missed at one such race when he did not show up. When walkers found the body of an elderly man in the bog, it was soon realised that he had met his end in the environment he loved so much.

It's a sad tale, and a harrowing one at that, but it's one that always comes to my mind when traversing boggy areas such as this, knowing full well they can catch out even the most experienced. After a few more leaps that were more akin to pole vaults courtesy of my walking apparatus, I reached the wall and, with no stile to help me, hauled my wet legs over the top of it. As this was the side I would ultimately need to be on to reach my goal, despite the much longer and tick-filled grass that awaited, I dutifully followed it uphill.

Almost immediately I began to get hot, heaving my waterlogged boots further and further up the steep slope, the ground sucking and gulping at my heels. I thought I could hear flowing water and momentarily risked switching on my head torch. There in front of me I was incredulous to see a drainage pipe that seemed to be pumping water out from the field I had just left and gushing it down into where I was standing. I turned the light off and continued upwards, resolute in my wet defeat. Then, to add insult to injury, I hit a wall. Not a mental one, you understand, as per a marathon runner around the 20-mile mark. No, this was a very real and physical stone wall blocking my way ahead. I sighed. I would have to go back into the other field I had just left.

Swinging on a metal gate to avoid most of the deep mud that had gathered in a thick wallow at its base, I went back into the short grass of the neighbouring pastureland, the air lit up with sheep eyes that seemed to dance around in the dark like bioluminescence in deep water. I was following what seemed to be the tracks of a quad bike. It made me laugh. So reluctant are they to have walkers damaging the land here with their boots, and scaring birds in the process, but quad bikes are an entirely different proposition. A little further up the obliterated field I hit a wall again, though this one was at least marked on the map. It was made of stone and at this gradient towered impossibly high – just in case I had any silly ideas, mind you, at its top was a sprawling length of barbed wire.

I looked at the wall to my right and spied a pile of stones on the floor. Whether or not they had been pulled out by walkers who had reached the same blockade as I had, I could not be sure, but I used this escape route and was instantly on the right side of the boundary once more. According to the map, from this point onwards I would climb a little at first and then undulate over bogs for a couple of kilometres until I came to the Whitendale Hanging Stones. I knew I would cover the distance slowly, not only because it was dark but also because of the necessary bog detours. Now, out of the sight line of any houses or farms, I turned on my head torch and vowed to not allow myself to stray so far right that I lost sight of the fence that should guide me to my goal. I decided to play it safe and set a half-hour timer on my watch; by the time it went off I should have reached a stile marked on the map – even allowing an extra 10 minutes for any detour.

Movement was indeed slow. Just as I managed to pick up momentum on some solid grass lumps, a giant, black peat hag would rise up from the ground in front of me, forcing me to walk out to the right to get around it. Sometimes I would have to go another hundred or so metres to find a way to penetrate it, other times I could see the steps from another walker who had been this way and burrowed into the sludge so I would use their footmarks to find purchase and heave myself up onto the top of it. But the fairly solid but slippery peat hags were just one of my problems. The worst was when what looked like solid soil would give way under my boot and send me plunging, my unprepared limb thrust deep into the bitterness of a pond. The peat stained everything. Shining my light down at my trousers, I could see I was caked in the stuff, as if on army manoeuvres. My hands were green and slimed from grabbing at the fence whenever bogs pulled just that little bit too vigorously on my feet. Though dark, the mist was still tangible, all around me like a thick veil.

I stood for a minute taking a breath and felt the inside of my pocket begin to vibrate – my alarm.

I hadn't reached where I wanted to be at this point, so I optimistically set another 10 minutes and began to plough on again. Voles or mice flitted about in the grass beneath my steps and occasionally I would hear the distinctive skin-flapping of bat wings, swooping and diving above my head. Just 5 minutes later I spotted the stile – I was on track, and the centre of Britain was now within my reach.

Back when the OS announced the centre of Britain to be officially the spot above Brennand Farm, I remember reading an interview with the owner of it, a Mr Walker, who had been at the place with his family since the seventies. He reflected philosophically on the news by saying he wished it had been on a hill instead, because then it would likely have been a bigger tourist attraction. As it is now, it's a long and – as I was fast finding out – slow trudge through less than ideal walking terrain.

The farm itself has some interesting history due to its remoteness. It's said that at the end of the First World War, so far flung and remote was it and its neighbouring Whitendale Farm from any good road, it took six weeks for news to reach the occupants that the fighting was over and the war had ended. Nowadays, with emails and texts, I'm sure it would happen a little sooner, but reading that fact still made me excited about coming to see this rarely talked-about area.

But, as with most places on my Extreme Sleeps Challenge, the war association didn't end there. Many areas of this blanket bog land and surrounding fells were used for training by the military, and rumours abound of unexploded bombs still lying in wait in some areas. That would be just my luck, I thought to myself as I jumped down yet another metre-tall peat hag. I find the centre of Britain and lay down my bivvy bag only to have the whole thing explode. Either that, I mused, or I would be lying in wait watching the grouse as they, like penguins in a Wallace and Gromit animation, ran unwittingly into the incendiary-device-laden ground and began exploding like fireworks in front of me.

Shaking this image from my head I yomped on, watching as my head torch illuminated a spider's web caked in dew, looking like a net of elegant Swarovski crystals. Attempting to make my way around another hag I stumbled upon a well-hidden grouse butt, so well disguised that the heather had even started to grow over the top of it. Nearby I saw what looked like a long piece of human excrement, it also coated in a glistening layer of web and water; a shooting party had clearly been here recently.

I climbed up away from it and stumbled into more mist. I checked the map again and set another timer, the previous one having come and gone – if I hadn't found the stones in another 10 minutes I would sleep wherever I could. No sooner had I set the timer and placed the phone back into my pocket, than the first wind-scoured stone presented itself to me.

The Whitendale Hanging Stones are an odd bunch of rocks. After kilometres and kilometres of anything but solid matter, they mushroom up from the ground all hard and striated. The first one sat quite low down to the ground, but there was ample room to squeeze myself alongside it if I needed to. I continued on to the next, only to find a series of about five such stones appearing in my head-torch light.

The first offered no obvious place to pitch next to, the second lacked shelter and the fourth and fifth were equally exposed, but the third, the third had a wonderful little nook, edged by tufts of long grass, with even a perfect shelf on which to rest my bag. This was the one.

An owl hooted somewhere nearby as I unfurled my bivvy bag. I blew up my mat quickly, eager to feel the warmth of my sleeping bag, and slipped inside. When I'd first seen the sign advising against camping I had been concerned that wild camping up here may be tricky and risky. But it was funny, up here I had never felt further away from anywhere – including when I had been in Fisherfield. I felt instantly at one with my surrounds, as though I blended in so completely that, even had someone been on my trail, sent out to look for this odd girl who was set on sleeping high on the moorland, I would have been almost impossible to find. Amid the calls of the grouse I never felt more alone, and lay with my eyes open in the darkness, waiting for light to come and find me.

I stayed like that for what seemed like hours, but at some point turned over and faced the protection of the cool overhanging rocks. My night was restless. I kept getting a draught around my neck and at one point I swear a sheep began trying to fight me for my space as the wind picked up in strong gusts, sending water spraying over my cheeks from the tips of the grass.

At some point I know I must have slept because I had a vivid dream about the man from Haltwhistle arguing with the man from Ordnance Survey about which point really was the true centre. One insisting his town had it first, the other methodically repeating that he had used a 'standard arithmetic principle' – a phrase I don't understand but had clearly read in my research, which had caused it to resurface in my subconscious – and explaining how even NASA used the same method.

I awoke in a grey light, similar to the one that I'd driven through to Dunsop Bridge. It didn't seem bright enough to mean I should leave the cocoon-like warmth of my bivvy and so I buried my face in my inflatable pillow and closed my eyes some more.

The area of Bowland is merely a representative patch of what's left of a great tract of wilderness that once covered most of England – including Hampshire's New Forest, Nottingham's Sherwood Forest and even Savernake Forest in Wiltshire. Of all the designated Areas of Outstanding Natural Beauty that abound within our shores, the Forest of Bowland is the one with very few visitors, which may help to explain in part the length of time it took for someone to discover the body of the poor late Bill Smith, and may also account for why I, alone at the centremost point of Britain, somehow managed to sleep in far too late without being disturbed. It was funny to think that here in the centre of Britain I felt more remote and further away from other human beings than I had at the other two extremities so far.

Perhaps that was why it was the feeling of being watched that made me stir, that and the growing number of calls from the grouse, no doubt rousing to a fury at the sight of this weird human-shaped intruder clogging up their landscape. I opened one eye to see a small bird of prey hovering a a couple of metres away from me, obviously having spotted something tasty lurking in the long grass.

The light was as nondescript as ever, not giving away any hint of what time of day I found myself in. I lay there in that half-light, a strange kind of mizzle surrounding everything, not exactly wet but not dry either. I surveyed my scene with the advantage of daylight, but even then the rocks appeared merely as faint tracings of apparitions in the mist. No matter how long I lingered, it seemed that the sun was going to remain an absent friend for me.

Though desolate and barren on first glance, the longer I stayed and watched, the more life I began to spot. From the rustle of a grouse to the stirrings of mice in the undergrowth, the place really was alive. And I also felt alive being here now, on my own, able to watch it all from my bed. How glad I was that the folks at Ordnance Survey had chosen the method they had to locate this place. How different my experience might have been. Had they included Northern Ireland, I might now be waking in the middle of Morecambe Bay, no doubt even wetter than I was now. If they'd chosen the place furthest from the sea I would find myself on farmland in Derbyshire. If they had chosen to go by the high tide mark I might by lying in a spot somewhere in Staffordshire. And, of course, if they'd gone with the midway point on the longest north–south axis to cut through the country then I would be, as many would prefer, waking up in Haltwhistle.

I rummaged inside my rucksack, suddenly remembering the camera, which I'd managed to charge just a little on my way here. Turning it on, I filmed this empty scene for many minutes, hoping to convey the sounds of life that lurked there despite appearances to the contrary.

'Go back! Go back!' came the call from my left – and, for once, it was right. I needed to head off now. No matter what time it was, I had definitely lingered too long in this place where time seemed to be on pause. If I were to carry on and possibly even complete my whole challenge, I had a fair way to go to reach my next sleep. I switched the camera off and began to pack my things away. I had quite a drive still ahead of me, one that would lead me further to the east.

CHAPTER TEN

LOWESTOFT NESS

'Can anyone tell me the name of the bird that has wings but does not fly and – it's not a penguin?' said the DJ on the local Radio Norfolk radio station. I flicked around with the frequency dial, and was immediately fed a torrent of mushy crooning love songs that even my gran would skip, followed by the inane thump-thump-thump of a rave track that could have been any one of several tracks currently doing the rounds. I turned back to Radio Norfolk to catch the end of a sentence '…in which we'll be asking you, what day of the week is worse than a Monday?'

I switched it off, the silence being an infinite improvement on my Alan Partridge-esque radio jockey. A few minutes later, though, I felt my eyelids begin to grow heavy again and, without fully realising it, I had returned to Radio Norfolk. 'Well, I've always hated Tuesdays,' came the crow of an elderly woman, 'it's like having Monday again but only worse…'

I looked at the clock on the dashboard; it was heading up to midnight. Just why this woman was up at this hour talking about days of the week was beyond me. I felt like I was eavesdropping on a private conversation that I had no business listening to, and which they didn't even seem to know anyone else might be listening to either – it was bizarre. Perhaps, though, I couldn't claim to be any less strange in my current activity. I myself was heading east. Not just east, but easter than east – the easternmost point there is, in fact, on mainland Britain. Known as Lowestoft Ness, it sits on the edge of a small town in the county of Suffolk, edging into the sea.

After my foray into the centre of this great country, I had decided to get a far-flung point of the compass ticked off next; only now was I beginning to realise just how far flung it was. As it was 270 miles from Dunsop Bridge (via the most direct route), I had worked out that it would take me around 4 hours to drive it.

When I had found my way out of the winding roads of the Forest of Bowland around lunchtime, I had thought I had ample time to get here. I had pootled around the landscape, oohing and ahhing at the wilderness beyond my windscreen. I had taken a detour to the luxury of a motorway to give my head a break from twists and turns. I had stopped for extra breaks at the multitude of service stations that line the A1, and I had even chanced a stroll down memory lane by taking the turn-off to Oundle in Northamptonshire, which I had frequently visited while stationed down the road in Peterborough several years previously.

It was only when I punched the coordinates into my satnav in no particular panic at around 8.30 p.m. that evening, while I ate my dinner at a roadside cafe on the A605, that I realised that the easternmost part of the country is – well, very far to the east.

Wolfing down my soup and roll, I jumped back behind the wheel of the car and got driving. As we edged nearer to December now, I was no longer shocked about the darkness. It seemed to come earlier each day, allowing me to do my challenge well under the cover of night, but as I left the main road and began driving on much more minor ones, in what seemed to be a courting ritual betwixt the counties of Norfolk and Suffolk, I did begin to despair. This was going to take a while.

Suffering a little already from having spent the last few nights not sleeping in a proper bed, I found this little road dance less than charming. I'd reached the Broads territory, crossing a network of streams, rivers and estuaries en route to the coast. In my tired state I began to become suspicious of anyone who was heading the same way as I was at this late hour. One car in particular seemed to have followed my exact route since we left the main road – and I was only blindly obeying the voice of Siri on my iPhone, so I had no idea what they were doing.

Town names came and went between radio conversations that were so inane I began to burst into fits of hysterics, believing someone to be purposefully manufacturing them purely for the amusement of late-night drivers like me.

As I flitted from Norfolk to Suffolk once more I spied a small service station, where the only place open was a McDonald's. The place I was heading to for my wild camp was going to be the most challenging on the whole trip. Not in terms of height or walking terrain, but because this spot was so close to civilisation. Lowestoft Ness and, more precisely, the spot of land called Ness Point sits at a longitude of 1 degree 45 minutes 53 seconds east. It is on the edge of a busy seaside town and as such very close to people's houses, workplaces and... nightclubs. In fact, this was to be the most urban wild sleep I had ever attempted.

That brought with it a whole new set of problems. The first was that all my gear was designed for high visibility on the mountains. One only had to cast a tiny section of light on it and the reflectors would bounce back like a big sign announcing my presence: 'Here I am, guys – I'm illegally camping.' Stealth was going to be tricky. The second problem was access. Sitting as it does in front of the sea, which, looking at the moon reflecting down on me like a giant crystal orb, was going to be at high tide, a sleep on the eastern edge may well be a wet one. Thirdly, this would be no place for lingering. This was to be a sleep only; no time to cook, eat snacks or unpack complicated kit marked in colour-coded bags, like I would do in the wilds. With this one, I had to pre-pack to make me stand out as little as possible and be completely ready to get into my bivvy and sleep immediately. Finally, and perhaps the biggest obstacle, was the need for a toilet. Unlike in the hills, I could not simply locate a discreet place in which to 'go'. Here I would be in a concrete, public place where public urination (and, of course, worse) would be distinctly frowned upon.

It was that final obstacle that made me pull over at McDonald's, which seemed to be a busy place. As I looked at my phone I suddenly realised it was also Friday night and that meant everyone inside but me was dressed to go out. Faces caked in make-up stared up as this bedraggled wild sleeper moseyed on in to their terrain. My hair was greasy and pulled back with a broken band. My T-shirt was the same base layer I had slept in for the last four nights; my face was coated by a layer of freckles around my nose that always seem to make an appearance when I've spent a prolonged period of time in the outdoors; and my trousers were thick with a mix of dried bog water and mud. I was in way out of my depth.

I swung into the toilets to find two girls a few years younger than me spraying their hair with lacquer and reapplying mascara. The air was thick with the scent of something resembling the Charlie Red that I too used to douse myself in when I was about 16. I smiled; they didn't. We were like two of the same species occupying very different worlds, they on the hunt for some nightlife dressed to the nines, me on the hunt for some nightlife dressed ready to go to sleep. They were in knee-high boots; I was sporting my three-season variety.

As I snuck out of the restaurant, the perfumed smell of the fast-food chain caught me in the throat as it always does; a combination of sweet and savoury, of something familiar yet desirable sent my head into a spin and set my stomach off growling. I made a dash for the door. In the car park huddles of boys lingered under the lights around their souped-up Ford Focuses, adorned with decals and spoilers to make them look like Cosworths from the rally tracks. The place was like a bizarre scene from a film about rival teen gangs. Here was where the groups of kids too young to be in pubs were opting to hang out, eating burgers and sipping milkshakes in some kind of skewered recreation of the 1950s.

I hurried back to my car and set off again, now within no more than 15 minutes of my destination; there was still time to reach it before midnight. Suddenly I was back in a country lane, the greenery lining my route with grandeur. Another turn and I entered what appeared to be a sprawling modern housing estate lit up like it was daytime under some powerful streetlights.

A girl who looked like she was either coming from or on her way to work walked briskly, looking over her shoulder. A little further on I saw movement in the hedgerow. Whatever it was jumped out in front of my car, forcing me to slam on the breaks and screech to a halt. Here in the middle of suburbia, a single, small muntjac deer ambled nervously across the tarmac, looking worried. Finally allowing myself to exhale a big gasp of air, I continued on, and a few seconds later I spotted the reason for its concern. A fox. Redder than the brickwork against which it moved under cover of, it watched my headlights speed by. I looked in my rear-view mirror to see him stalking the deer, weaving its body between the ferns, the flash of its white tail seen only as a glimpse before I lost him and the muntjac into the night.

Amused that my most impressive wildlife encounter to date had happened on my most urban of sleeps, I continued on to a set of lights where signs directed me to the town centre. I was still yet to see the sea; it seemed that any glimpse of it had been bricked up by the needs of modern development.

I would have to wait a good while yet. Soon I was plunged head first into a busy Friday night, with neon signs flashing outside takeaways and nightclubs. People were spilling, inebriated, out of what looked like a former church – now a trendy nightspot. Some ran over to my car, attempting to flag me down, convinced I was a passing taxi; I locked my doors. This was going to be the hardest sleep in my challenge.

Whether it was nerves I don't know, but suddenly I found myself needing the toilet yet again. I drove around looking for somewhere that was open – a garage, a takeaway, anything – but found nothing. I was going to have to wait.

Holding the title of the easternmost point of mainland Britain you'd think that Ness Point would be something of a well-publicised tourist attraction. Sadly for it, that isn't the case. The point which marks the easternmost bearing is a large compass-like circle on the ground, called a Euroscope. I had seen pictures of it during my research, when I had also stumbled across a newspaper article, penned in 2008, which bemoaned the lack of initiative in inviting tourists to come and see it. Of all the compass points it's by far the most accessible, but it also has the least to recommend it to visitors, as I was currently finding out as I trawled the main street that ran alongside the promenade, trying with all my navigational nous to find the bloody waterfront.

If I stopped and rolled down my window I could hear the distant crashing of the waves, so I knew it was here somewhere, but every time I thought I was getting nearer a one-way sign led me on a not uninteresting diversion around houses I had not seen before, after which it deposited me back on a street I'd seen at least ten times before, and then the whole process would start all over again. It didn't seem to make any difference at which point I turned off that street, somehow I would always end up back there, the sound of the sea in my ears but its location still locked away by the buildings. I stopped again and tried to locate myself on the map on my phone. Before I could properly plot my next move I heard loud blasts of music from the nightclubs and watched as a door opened in a building a few metres from where I'd stopped and a group of people emerged laughing and talking loudly. Knowing that it wouldn't be long before they attempted to hail me to take them home, I sped off, now determined on my course for the ocean.

Coming up to a little roundabout I had swung past several times before, this time I took an immediate left as though I was heading for what looked like nothing more than an industrial estate.

The streets here were dark and uncrowded, not like those on the high street just a block or two away. I wound down my window a little, letting the cold night air breeze inside my warm interior. Somewhere nearby I could hear the low and constant murmur of machinery. A smell, familiar and yet vastly unpleasant, began to ooze into my nostrils. I instinctively began to wind up the window, but it was too late. The greasy scent of fried fish engulfed the car; I could even taste it in the back of my throat. Where was it coming from?

Less than a minute later I was confronted with it. Birds Eye. The frozen-food manufacturer's base was sprawled over street after street in front of me. Through the glass I could make out the shapes of the workers inside, clad head to toe in blue overalls as they cooked and froze the nation's ready-meals. Above the buildings rose several chimneys, and each one pumped out the fishy smell that was now making me retch. I looked down at my map. Between me and my sleep for the night stood one thing and one thing only; this factory.

I drove around it with all the stealth of a boy racer, trying to find an access point. My Google map was trying to persuade me to turn into the factory gates where a security guy sat in a little booth – that was clearly out of the question. So I drove back the other way. Soon I came to another factory, though this one had all the lights switched off. The end of the road was here too, but an array of 'No parking' signs warned me off and that, coupled with a number of CCTV cameras pointed decidedly at my car, made me realise that this was not the prime way in. As I performed yet another U-turn I noticed the employees of a taxi office on the corner beginning to become suspicious, with the one smoking a cigarette on the doorstep now gesturing to his colleagues to come and take a look.

Not wanting to attract attention I drove on, giving up on finding an easier access point to the waterfront. I pulled up and parallel parked in front of the Birds Eye factory among the workers' cars. I wasn't sure what time their shifts would end, but no one appeared to be lingering at the doors. I sat still, willing the internal light in my vehicle to switch off, it seeming to take an unnecessary age to do so.

Finally, now coated in a blanket of darkness, I set to work. I pulled out my bivvy and stuffed my sleeping bag inside it ready. Pulling my rucksack from the passenger seat I emptied its contents into the footwell and pulled out just three items – my down jacket, my head torch and my hat. One by one I put them on, placing the head torch around my neck, and cursed the fact that my jacket was a near luminous shade of blue. Thinking better of it, I removed it and instead pulled on my black fleece. Between it and my trousers I looked like I might be planning some kind of heist – me on a mission to steal a recipe from Britain's best-loved frozen-food manufacturer. I replaced the empty space in my rucksack with my ready-packed bivvy bag and, grabbing the video camera as a final afterthought, I left the safety of the car.

The smell hit me yet again; my retch reflex still reacting to it. I hurried along the pavement, trying to get a look at any weak points where I might sneak through to reach the sea. Nothing. As the building ended I saw with delight that a wide expansive playing field – or at least an area of grass the size of a playing field – extended down to the sea wall. I could make it; this was my way in. The grass was pretty treacherous to cross. Never mind the bogs and peat of the Forest of Bowland, this seemed to be littered with ankle-breaking potholes. I stumbled my way across in the dark, unwilling to give up my position too easily to anyone who might be watching by turning on my head torch. Halfway across I reached a huge window into the factory and impulsively ducked down and began to crawl beneath it. As I did so, I looked to my left across the grass.

I could just make out the white tail of a rabbit – no doubt one of those responsible for making the sea of holes I was crossing. I stood up once more, then made a final dash for the sea wall. Even from here I could hear the waves crashing against it, and by way of confirmation when I reached it, a huge spray of salt water splashed over the side, covering me head to toe in brine. The ocean was definitely on the other side.

The wall up to the promenade was slanted at a strange angle, just too steep to make it an easy walk, but not steep enough to rule it out as impossible. I placed one foot on it first and felt my boot grip firmly on the pebble stone. I leaned my whole body over to join it, my two hands making contact with it and, finally, my other foot. Managing to hold traction despite the constant splash of water tumbling down it, I edged crab-like up to the top. Who would have thought an urban sleep could have been this hard?

Finally, the edge of a small vertical wall was within reach at the top. I grabbed it and hoisted myself up onto it, my legs running up the final metre of the slope. I stood triumphantly on the top and promptly got a mouthful of seawater.

Stepping over the small wall that had helped me up, I was now on the promenade proper and, not wanting to forget myself, I did a little piece to camera saying how difficult this thing had been to master. Beneath a second small wall I could see that the tide was well and truly in, the surf crashing mercilessly against the breakwater shapes below, frothing violently with each upsurge. I stood watching it for several minutes, trying to grasp its ferocity and work out if it was coming in any further. Every few waves a huge breaker would cover the whole promenade and pull back any loose debris with it, be it rocks or seaweed. This was starting to look impossible.

I turned my back on that problem for a moment and pulled out my phone to check the map. I was still a little way from the true easternmost point, and I needed to head south. I began to walk along the promenade, which now passed directly in front of the floodlit factory. In the forecourt area I passed first, one worker was operating a machine lifting pallets and, focused intently on the job at hand, seemed to pay me no heed. Behind the window of the area next to it were three workers, lost deep in a conversation, a radio (no doubt Radio Norfolk) blaring behind them. They also failed to spot me. I hurried along, thinking just how I would convince any suspicious security guards that I was on a mission to sleep and not to discover the secret ingredient of their infamous fish finger. The distance was not far but felt it in my exposed position, and I found myself edging further towards the waves rather than risk being questioned by Captain Birds Eye and the gang.

Finally I escaped the glare of the factory lights and became somewhat concealed in the darkness once more. Despite the constant salty spray covering me every so many steps I was surprised to feel warm. The thermometer in the car had read 9.5°C, so compared to my other sleeps, with no rain falling on me, this was indeed the hottest.

As I neared my goal of the easternmost point I was amazed to see a huge wind turbine pulsating around and around, towering above the business premises it seemed to belong to. On my return home, a bit of reading into this other industrial monstrosity revealed it to be the site of the Orbis Energy Centre – a renewable energy business centre. On its land sits – wait for it – Britain's tallest wind turbine. Standing a whopping 126 metres, those looking further into its background will find that it is responsible for generating energy for the National Grid, and is affectionately nicknamed Gulliver.

With the smell of deep-fried frozen fish stinging my nostrils, salt water stinging my ears and the surrounds – it has to be said – insulting my eyes, I set about working out just where I might be able to pitch camp. I looked down to the Euroscope, the huge black-and-white disc that lies on the ground of Ness Point. Even from my vantage point above I couldn't see it clearly, as giant waves of high tide continued to flood it completely, only its westernmost edges occasionally peeking out underneath.

When looking up information about this easternmost point after my visit, I stumbled upon a campaign started by the local radio station and their news team seven years ago, imploring the Waveney District Council to make something of their quirky landmark.

One of their points I could definitely attest to is that it is woefully difficult to find, with no signs advertising 'The most easterly point in Britain' anywhere along the way (apparently there are signs to lead you to Ness Point, but I confess I couldn't find those either). Another point the campaigners made was that the road leading to it – I later rather guttingly found out that an unmarked road just opposite the taxi office I sped away from takes you to the promenade just below it! – should be changed from its unappealing 'Gasworks Road' moniker to something more appealing like 'Sunrise Lane'.

Another point the author of the news story made was that a sign at the point wouldn't go amiss either. He comically wrote: 'To take a photograph you have to lie flat on the Euroscope dial, which floods at extremely high tide.' Again I can back him up on this one. He also called for an interpretation board – still absent – then ends spectacularly with the sentence: 'Seats that actually face out to sea would be good, not like the ones there now, which you can only sit on looking inland at the septic interceptor!'

That's right, a septic interceptor does indeed stand above the easternmost point in Britain, merely metres away from Britain's tallest wind turbine. For anyone feeling I'm being unfair at this point, I will make one concession. Since that article was penned, the campaigners have secured one small victory; those seats now do face out to sea.

I did for one minute consider that I might try a sleep on one of them, but I quickly dismissed it, thinking it would be crossing the line from wild sleeper to homeless person. Besides, a streetlight very visibly lit them up and should anyone have come into the car park below – which at this point I still believed to be an employee car park for workers at Birds Eye or Orbis Renewable Energy – I would be the first thing they would see.

With the Euroscope quite literally a washout and the bench far too blatant, I began to search for an easterly Plan B. First I walked down towards the Euroscope on the sloping walkway and a massive wave, carrying with it several large stones, exploded on the ground in front of me. Getting close to the sea would be too dangerous. I edged along the prom a little and near the end of the buildings sheltered by the sea wall and hidden by some greenery I was presented with the only option open to me.

I looked about me; the constant circling of the lighthouse beam high up on a hill provided me with some light; the fluorescent blaze of tungsten strip lighting and outdoor high-visibility beams lit up the workers; and the air wafted the fishy smell in and out of my nose. And so it was there, very unglamorously, beneath a septic interceptor in the lee breeze of the Birds Eye factory, that I settled down for my easternmost sleep. With so much light pollution around me, I barely needed my head torch to scope out the ground below me before committing to my patch. A quick sweep of it confirmed that I was not the first to lie here – though maybe the first to do so with the intention of sleeping. A discarded belt, some used tissue paper and an empty bottle of whisky all had to be kicked away with my boot first. I climbed into my bivvy back unenthused, wondering why on earth I was doing this challenge in the first place.

I wouldn't say I slept so much as rested my eyes and dozed a little. I set my alarm for 6.30 a.m., by which time I would have completed my necessary hours and it would still be dark enough and early enough that no one should happen upon me. I never did get used to the smell from the factory, but I tried instead to focus on the sounds of the crashing waves and imagine myself to be anywhere other than where I was.

I was jolted awake at around 2 a.m., when I swore I saw the flashing red light from what appeared to be a bicycle on the other side of the car park. I stared at it through my tired eyes, trying to force myself to focus. It seemed to be circling around in a giant figure of eight. I watched it for a few minutes, wondering if the rider knew I was there. It stopped a couple of times and I braced myself for discovery, feeling enclosed, vulnerable in my bivvy bag, too close to civilisation for comfort. But then it would start again and I would begin to breathe. I had not been seen. At one point I pulled out the video camera and switched it to night mode and attempted to zoom in, trying to capture the owner, but it was no use, the camera either wouldn't focus on them or there was no them to focus on. I put it away and closed my eyes tightly again.

The scurry of something furry nearby spooked me about an hour afterwards. I swore I caught the glare of a rabbit's eyes meeting mine, and tried to pretend that they weren't, in actual fact, those of a rat.

The sound from the wind turbine, the constant hum of which I didn't really hear at first over the chinks and clamping sounds of the frozen-food factory, made me open my eyes a little after 4 a.m., the wind still blowing hard. Wide awake, I made a little dash to look over the sea wall and watched the breaking waves, which had now started to move away from the land. The twinkling lights of the ships at sea bobbed on the horizon.

With that happier picture in my mind, I climbed back into bed and didn't wake again until my alarm went off, its vibrations shaking up the hand which clasped it firmly in my grip, the tune so quiet in this place that I couldn't even decipher it.

When I emerged from the bush, with my bivvy bag safely stowed away, a taxi was waiting in the car park about 20 metres away from me. I don't think he was there to collect a fare; rather he was sitting, calmly staring out towards the sea. From his position he wouldn't have been able to see it – indeed, I couldn't from where I stood – but I do think there's something about the sounds of the sea, and the knowledge that the coast is there, which have a truly calming effect.

The familiar caw of the seagulls overhead, gliding and bouncing effortlessly on the wind, took me instantly back to my childhood on the North Wales coast. Gulliver, the wind turbine that had looked so ugly to me in the night, now reminded me fondly of the little plastic windmills we would plant in the top of our sandcastles on the beach. I climbed up to the promenade again and went and sat on the bench. The sky glowed white, sporting a rosy blush in these early-morning hours. Now the waves had retreated to a point where the remains of an old jetty or boat ramp stretched down to them, several metres beyond the Euroscope.

Washed clean from a night of wave battering, the Euroscope itself was also coated in a peach-like sheen from the sun. It was a warm morning and rain so far had held off.

I walked down to stand in its centre, where a metal disc simply says 'Lowestoft', then 'Britain's most easterly point'. It was clear and to the point, but at that moment it made me smile. I walked north on it to find it naming Dunnet Head as the northernmost point. I continued round the circumference, spotting Lizard Point – which would be my final stop on this challenge – and then west, which incorrectly named Ardnamurchan Point as the westernmost point. I shook my head at this error, though secretly I was glad, not wanting too many others to seek out my favourite campsite of the lot so far.

Still groggy from my restless sleep, I looked about me. I may have felt a little queasy from the smell of the factory, a little tired from the briny air that still whipped up the sea water into pounding waves below the promenade, but I had to say, with the sun beginning to rise in front of me and casting the whole scene in the ethereal pinkish tone of an impressionist painting, there were certainly worse places to wake up.

And I wasn't alone. The taxi driver had got out of his car and now sat on the bench above, not needing a paper or mobile phone to occupy his time, just staring contentedly at the sea. Further along the prom a couple meandered slowly along with their dog, happy in each other's company. And behind them a runner used the high walkway above the waves to start a Saturday fresh in the elements.

A few days after I had left Lowestoft Ness I looked it up online to see that Suffolk County Council and Waveney District Council were hopeful of working out an effective way to bring more tourists to the easternmost point of mainland Britain.

And, as I sat in the centre of the Euroscope, drinking it all in, watching the thin slit of light pierce its way through the grey clouds, signifying dawn, I felt hopeful too, not only for my challenge to be completed, but also for the future of this eastern extremity.

CHAPTER ELEVEN

HOLME FEN

Before leaving Lowestoft Ness I realised that it would only take a couple of hours to head west to my next wild sleep in Huntingdonshire, at a place called Holme Fen, the lowest place in mainland Britain. Having woken early by the sea, and after lingering for a while, pacing the promenade and finding an unexpected wild beauty in the churning waves alongside all the man-made industrial buildings, I had stayed on to have my breakfast in one of the cafes and didn't bother leaving until a little after 10 a.m. Today, time was not an enemy with which I had to do battle. Now I had plenty of it, too much in fact, and it was going to be difficult to fill it.

First I decided to take advantage of my limited winter hours of daylight and recce my chosen sleep spot before I went there at night – a luxury I rarely afford myself, even though I always advise others to do so when wild camping.

Though I had lived near this spot for nearly four years of my life, I had never actually been to it before. Sitting at an 'elevation' of approximately 2.75 metres below sea level, a small spot of ground within the woodland of Holme Fen is officially the lowest place there is in our country and – rumour has it – it may sink further.

What is now a nature reserve within the East Anglian Fens was once a network of shallow lakes and tarns that floated amongst the peat, rather than the solid land you see today. We humans couldn't work with land like this used to be – it would be like trying to build or farm high up in the Forest of Bowland, a thankless task. And so the fens were systematically drained to make the lands within them viable to work on.

The River Nene, which today stretches from Northampton in the west to meet the Wash in the east, used to flow through one of the old lakes (Whittlesey Mere) before heading up to the River Ouse. That was until 1851, when these large bodies of water were drained to expand the peat. The great mere of Whittlesey was reduced to about 400 hectares from 1200 hectares, with a depth of just 1 metre. Later that same year the remaining water was carried away using a drainage system.

For farmers this plan worked out well. With the pools of water gone, what remained became arable farmland.

I could certainly see evidence of all this as I left the A1(M) and began my trek across country roads, my course set for the tiny hamlet of Holme. With a population of around 700, there's not a lot of entertainment in the form of shops or landmarks to attract people to this part of the world. There are, however, plenty of farms. And in the few miles I drove to reach Holme, I saw one after the other, the fields looking well tended and no doubt producing a range of crops that bring their owners or tenants a good livelihood.

Eventually I reached the outskirts of the small stronghold, passing a primary school, church and village hall as I weaved around its roads. On the corner sat a single pub called the Admiral Wells, but at this early hour not a soul stirred inside or out. A little further and a line of cars made me stop. I had reached the railway tracks and, as they are main lines that take passengers from Peterborough and beyond down into London, the crossings frequently cause traffic jams as motorists are forced to stop for several trains at a time.

Now the red lights flashed on and off and we waited for three different trains to cross in front of us. The veneer of the carriages seemed out of place somehow amid the flatness and greenery of the fens and fields that surrounded us. When the barriers lifted, I followed my map around to the little nature reserve that makes up Holme Fen. It was late morning and I was surprised to see that there was nowhere to park; all the spaces at the lay-by were taken. I double-parked and walked to the edge of it, where the long grass reached as high as my chest. I looked at my map to find another way in.

Jumping back in my car I approached another farm and then made a left turn over a dirt-encrusted single-track tarmac road back towards the fen. This road seemed to dissect the forest in two, and as I pulled up at the lay-by to claim the last space as my own, I realised that the forest on the left was the half I wanted, as signified by the presence of two large, green metal posts.

Back when the peaty mire was still flooded in the early 1800s, the landowner at Holme Fen – a man named William Wells – had the foresight to realise that the land would subside once it had lost its water and therefore its structural integrity.

To prove it, he took a post make of oak and planted it firmly in the clay that sits beneath the peat. He then cut the top of it off, so that all that remained was below ground. This would be his makeshift peat-level monitor. The wood that became exposed could be measured to show the amount of land that had been lost.

Some years after he did this the oak post was replaced by a cast-iron column, alleged to have come from the Crystal Palace built to house the Great Exhibition of 1851. Pains were taken to make sure that this metal post matched up with the level of the original wooden one in order to maintain the accuracy of the record. As the years passed, the peat levels continued to sink. In 1957 steel support rods needed to be added and at that same time a second post was added alongside it. And it's these two posts – known as the Holme Posts – that are still visible today.

And my, are they visible. A shocking 4 metres above ground, in fact. As I neared them on foot, I thought it was my distant perspective that made them look so large, but as I made my way yet closer they towered over me. Once at their base, I felt dwarfed by them. Though William Wells never lived to see them sticking out of the ground this much, I wondered if he had ever imagined that the subsidence would reach down to such a level when he first planted his wooden post.

Fresh from my nightshift in Suffolk, I felt tired so decided to take a stroll through the woodland to familiarise myself with the place that would be my bedroom later on that evening. No matter where I go in Britain to walk in woodland it seems to share the same glorious scent, that damp and slightly mouldy smell of decaying leaves. When I was a little girl I used to live in a house that sat below a patch of woodland. In the daytime, especially during the summer holidays, I and a friend who lived down the road would go into it and stay hidden under its canopy until we had to return home at teatime. We would spend the hours making dens in the roots, sweeping the floor with broom-like branches, attempting to climb the large oaks, and playing hide and seek unperturbed by the coolness felt away from the sunlight. While I remember the games we played, the conversations we had I have forgotten, lost as casualties of time, vanished like the disintegrated leaves crushed under a walker's boots. But I can remember that smell, that ever-familiar scent of the woodland – like camomile tea – and in an instant I am transported back there, back to carefree days in the friendly woods, and I am happy.

I meandered now through the trees, trying hard to imagine how it would have looked here back in 1850 before man quite literally pulled the plug on the water that flowed through. At that time you could have sailed boats on the mere and, according to the interpretation board, they actually did, once holding a regatta on it.

I looked down at my feet, the soles of my shoes caked in peat, a thick black line of mush all about them. Peat is a funny thing. To the untrained eye it just looks like very dark, very thick mud. But that mud is very special. Forming over thousands of years from the remains of plants, it not only helps remove poisonous carbon dioxide from the earth's atmosphere, it also feeds an abundance of native wildlife, including the many birds and plants for which the area is famous. The fen woodrush that grows here is only found in this part of Britain and nowhere else beyond it. Peat doesn't just feed wildlife either, it helps feed us too. Enabling farmers to grow crops like carrots and potatoes, it was heralded by some as 'black gold'. Now it seems, with peat disappearing at a rate of knots, we may have to sacrifice some of this crop-bearing land and let it return to its natural state to help the peat recover.

I paced slowly and assuredly through the woodland, spotting the bark of silver birch, alder and oak trees. Twigs seemed to crack all around me as the landscape became alive at a micro level beneath my boots. I walked past a felled tree branch which was already beginning to be broken down by the forest, its bark moist and chipping away, a collection of white fungi growing within it, new life finding its way within the old.

I decided to follow a track of the old gamekeeper's plantation, taking in a roughly square section of the forest. I walked noisily as leaves fell down either side of me, a kind of natural ticker tape parade welcoming me deeper into its heart. Where the path reached a T-junction I spotted something in a clearing just ahead of me. There sat an old copper-looking cauldron; the charcoal bin.

It was here during the Second World War that they decided to clear away some of the woodland and use the peat to manufacture charcoal right here on this very spot – another surprising wartime connection. Since then the forest has started to reclaim the man-made structure. Inside it the roots and stems of a mixture of trees and stinging nettles had caused the bottom to fall out and the sides were overgrown with shrubbery, leaving very little of the metal still visible. According to the interpretation panel at the start of my stroll, a resident called Tony Redhead, who lived in nearby Tower Farm at the time the charcoal was made, reported that the process seemed to attract a feathery visitor to Holme Fen who had not been there before; the nightingale.

I continued on my walk, kicking up loose leaves as I went. It seemed funny to imagine any kind of manufacturing going on here now. Despite the cars I'd seen, which told me that there were other visitors in this pretty piece of man-kept wilderness, I still hadn't seen another soul.

I turned off the main path and down a particularly sodden passageway of trees, some still clinging to their red and brown leaves, others shedding theirs as I stepped by. It was a glorious smell that tickled my nose hairs, the scent of autumn, of old life making way for new life. I couldn't wait to return here when it got dark.

Before I headed off I crossed the road over to Burnham's Mere for a glimpse of how things used to look. The water moved and swirled in the winds, reflecting the leafy landscape occasionally. In spring and summer I could imagine that the place would be alive with waterbirds and insects, the great crested glebes showing off their elaborately ornate headdresses, mallards quacking around the edges, dragonflies soaring and skimming the surface of the lake. When you really think about it, the human race may have worked hard to destroy many a landscape, but we can be good at maintaining and protecting them too, as we were clearly doing with Burnham's Mere.

Taking one last look at the Holme Posts, I got back into my car and left, knowing that I would be back to sleep later. My daytime meandering now took me into an environment I'd been out of the habit of visiting, especially amidst the throngs of a busy Saturday. I had nipped into the city of Peterborough to grab something hot to eat and quickly wished I hadn't.

Bustling through the masses, fighting my way through to pay, it was a far cry from the peacefulness of the forest.

Heading back outside I drove over to another beauty spot, one near the river in Oundle. However, on pulling up I spotted the rather steep parking charge and, as I could park for free at the equally beautiful spot I had my sights set on for tonight's challenge, I decided to move on. My day continued like this, seeking out constant distractions. I parked up on a side road somewhere in the country and decided to follow the river there for an hour, to see where and how far I could get before I had to turn back. I stopped at a coffee shop and managed to while away an hour nursing my brew and reading the weekend papers, while watching people walk by. And then things got really desperate. With time ticking on, and feeling reluctant to go to sleep before the clock had even reached double figures, I went to a service station.

The services seemed instantly too bright, too busy. I felt completely out of my depth. There everyone seemed hell-bent on a specific purpose, be it get a coffee and hit the road, wolf down a sandwich or freshen up in the toilets – I even remembered the last time I was here, using this very place to get ready for a job interview at a walking magazine after I had made the long journey over here from Wales. I never realised at the time it would see me staying in this neck of the woods for the next four years. Now I felt aimless, wandering from one concession stand to the next, not even really hungry, just bored.

In a way, this whole experience of sleeping at the extremities of Britain had morphed into something else. Sure, the sleeps themselves were an important factor, but the time in between sleeps became equally as important. The act of getting from one sleep to another was an extra element, every bit as much a part of my adventure. The journeys became as important as the destinations themselves and this culminated in one thing: service stations (or the lack of service stations). They had become very much part of my daily routine. The busy hubbub of these temporary human shelters spaced evenly along roadsides contrasted starkly with my moments away from other people.

They all offered something different and also, at the same time, some similarities. There were the bigger ones, whose adverts seemed targeted at a very particular type of customer – usually the type with a weak bladder. Did you know that 'overactive bladder' is a condition that affects at least one in three women over the age of 45? Then there were the smaller ones, which seemed to care more about other people's well-being, their ads depicting children in Africa encouraging you to twin your toilet with theirs or to donate just £5 a month to the cause. In the more local stops down south, the increased charge to cross the Dartford Crossing seemed to be the hot topic of conversation, whereas on the northern borders with Scotland the favoured topic was the new law that would seek to criminalise anyone having more than a whiff of alcohol in their bloodstream if they were driving. In the north staff seemed friendly all told, compared to the south, and here in the outer reaches of Peterborough they just seemed bemused.

'Are you sure you don't want fries with that?' the attended asked as he placed my rather unusual order of a cheeseburger – no meat – on the counter, alongside my extra-large cup of tea. It was a little after 11 p.m. and I was still trying hard to kill time. They build these service stations to be so alike so as not to disorientate the tired driver, with the result that it's often difficult in your brain-addled fuzz to work out just where you are exactly. The one I was in now was the spitting image of one I'd been to on the M11 near Cambridge, for example (but I was pretty certain I was no longer there), and that one was a virtual carbon copy of one I'd encountered near a turn-off for the M25. I took my food and sat at a table, my brain a blur of single-serve conversations, name tags, fast food, streetlights, reflective signs and 'do not park here' warnings.

I couldn't wait to get out. I was tired and dreaming of a comfy pillow, but also longing to get to something less urban. Soon I left, and once more I made a beeline for Holme Fen, this time under the cover of night.

I drove a different way to get there this time, to take out the section on the motorway. Driving through the village of Yaxley, I watched in disbelief as the air began to grow thick with a night fog. I had almost forgotten this phenomenon of the fens, an occurrence when, even late at night, a thick mist can suddenly descend, making the famously big skies of Norfolk close in and feel quite claustrophobic.

I left the last of the houses behind, the light cast on the road from their windows disappearing, replaced only with darkness. I turned my lights on to high beam, but that seemed to make visibility even worse, the beams themselves reflecting off the mist and near blinding me.

I made my way cautiously along the road; with high grass either side I did not want to be responsible for hitting an animal that decided to dart out suddenly. I watched my satnav map like a hawk, so that I would be prepared whenever a bend in the road came up.

I looked up into my rear-view mirror, then did a double-take – there was a car behind me. Once more I went into a paranoid, delusional state, thinking that someone was following me, for surely I was the only person daft enough to be out on this country lane so late at night. To be on the safe side, I purposely missed my turn-off and drove in to the village of Holme. I passed the Admiral Wells and was surprised to see that the car park was rammed full of vehicles, the people eating and drinking inside illuminated against the windows – who'd have thought such a far-flung place would do so well? Then I reminded myself that this was Saturday night, after all.

As I drove around the village further – just to confuse anyone who might be taking notice of me – I passed Holmewood Hall, a Victorian structure that now serves as a rentable training centre, but during the Second World War was the location of the headquarters of the US Office of Strategic Services, where they packed the containers that would be parachuted into Europe to help supply the anti-Nazi resistance groups with whatever they needed.

I detoured back out of the main village, heading towards the motorway. Then, when the coast was clear, I headed back in one last time, now determined to make it to Holme Fen. As I went past the village sign once more, I noticed that it depicted a man leading a carthorse alongside a canal, apparently towing a floating church. Later I found out that there had indeed been a mobile holy place on a barge, designed by the Reverend George Broke, who served as the rector of this village in the late eighteenth and early nineteenth centuries. It was his means of delivering church services to those areas of the Fens that were otherwise cut off by winter floods.

I drove straight through the village now and turned down the road that meets the train tracks. Here I was stopped by the red flashing lights and forced to wait once more as the series of three trains thundered on by, each carriage that passed seemingly a hub of activity bathed in the glow of white light.

I drove on, noting that any vehicles that had been parked here earlier had now all left. I pulled up into the main lay-by and turned off my lights, waiting one more time for the internal lights in the car to dim to nothing, trying again to envisage the lake that was once the main feature of my surroundings for the night.

When they bled Whittlesey Mere dry I read that they used a pump which was first shown at the Great Exhibition in the Crystal Palace, quite a coincidence when you consider where the first cast-iron column that marked Britain's lowest point came from. Despite much local protest against losing the water, the plans went ahead with the agreement of the landowners, and the great lake, once used by royals for 'floating picnics', was no more.

I looked at the pretty cluster of trees from my window, all dark and skeletal in the night sky. The moon appeared as a fuzzy smear in the distance, but it was enough to light up the road next to which I sat. When they removed the water by force in 1851 they found a few spoils at the bottom, including an incense boat and a sword, which are said to have tipped off a large barge as it made its way to Ramsey Abbey to the south-east, and which now sit in the Victoria and Albert Museum in central London. They were fools, I decided, as I readied my bag for this night's escapade. The real treasure was right under their noses the whole time – and they pumped it away in the name of progress. I stepped out into the dark.

At night everywhere looks different, and that small patch of woodland around Holme Fen was no exception. Once friendly and familiar by day, now under the thicket of night it took on a much more sinister turn. I knew I would be safely concealed by the trees and the night sky, but then so could someone else be, lurking in the undergrowth. I felt around in my pocket for the reassuring metal handle of the camping knife I had with me. As I did so, I lost my footing on the bridge, made slick with moisture from the evening air, and skidded into a puddle on the other side. I couldn't help but laugh at myself. Here I was, worried about people lurking in shadows, when I was in fact the biggest danger to myself out here. I let go of the knife in my pocket and continued forward, merging into the darkness of the forest.

Unsurprisingly, soon after the pumping out of the water basin, the former site of the mere flooded – almost immediately, in fact, in 1852, at which point the landowners opted to drain it once more by pump. The same thing happened again 11 years later, when a sluice upriver gave up and the water flooded back in, the liquid seemingly remembering its rightful home.

It didn't last long, of course. That too was redrained and now the only thing that remains as testament to the great lake that once stood here is a mention on the maps of the area: 'Whittlesey Mere', even though the water is long gone.

I walked up to the first metal post and touched it with my fingers, the moisture already gathered in the creases in its metalwork. I pulled out my video camera and turned it on, knowing I didn't have the luxury of shooting too much within the diminished battery life. I cringed as the bright light from the screen seemed to blaze out in the night. Switching it to night mode, I turned it to face me, lined my face up into the shot and began talking, realising that I was only whispering without meaning to.

When I had run out of things to say I walked around the fence. I began seeking the spot I had found earlier in the daylight. Just a few metres back from the posts a large tree had fallen and the ground underneath was made soft from the soil that was blanketed in dead leaves and bouncy peat.

I left the path and was forced to turn on my head torch. As I did so, something leapt away into the bushes. A fox? A badger, perhaps? Something large enough to make it sound like a little bit of a commotion, but small enough to simply disappear into the foliage.

As I found my spot, marked by the fact that a sizable trunk now blocked my route forward, I lay down my cut-up survival bag first and patted it down on the ground, feeling for anything sharp or bumpy that would make my night less comfortable. After a bit of nesting I lay down my bivvy and sleeping mat in one go, took off my boots and snuggled inside my bag, waiting for the noise I was making to stop sounding so loud in the dead silence.

In an effort to remain disguised to any passers-by, I had also brought with me a black bin bag, and now used it to house my rucksack. Now, at least, no colours would give me away.

In a way I was lucky to be getting away with this now. The partnership that looks after this National Nature Reserve is currently lobbying for permission to build a visitor's centre here, claiming that, as it currently stands, Holme Fen is too small to get funding and remain protected. Instead, they want to combine it with Woodwalton Fen to create the new, larger reserve of Great Fen. If successful, the combined area's visitor centre would be a little over a couple of kilometres away from where I was now.

I understood what they were trying to do and certainly, to me, working to protect a wild place is admirable, but it seemed somehow at odds with the general aims, that to protect a wild space you first have to make it safe and friendly for humans, with a toilet and a cafe. Why can't we just preserve it as is, without the need for such modern conveniences?

Enjoying my time for now, without having to worry about the opening times of the gift shop, I rested my head, drinking in the smells of the forest and slowly, steadily, allowing myself to shut down and drift slowly and peacefully into a wonderful sleep, which, I could say without any real scientific proof or hard mathematical fact, was even deeper below sea level than the ground at the two Holme Posts.

I woke about half an hour later, shaken rudely from my slumber by what I thought was thunder. I realised by the time the second one went by that it had actually been the 12.26 service to London Euston.

I dozed again for a little while, then heard a twig or something break and woke with a jolt, sitting up and nearly cracking my head on the felled tree trunk overhead that was acting as my natural shelter.

Later, it was a digging sound over my left shoulder that stirred me. The noises of the night became a whole orchestral playing of woodland sounds – rustling leaves, squeaking soil sediments, the drifting sound of leaves falling from the trees. I may have been trying to sleep, but around me the whole forest was coming to life. It was as though the leaves had taken on a personality of their own and the trees began to creak in conversation with each other. I chanced to open my eyes and saw that many metres above my head, high in the darkness of night above the forest, one by one leaves were falling from tree branches – the autumnal mass suicide that leaves make in order to preserve the trunk. It was painstakingly beautiful; I shut my eyes again.

In recent years – going back to around 2002 – plans were in the pipeline to save the subsiding peat which the wildlife here so heavily relies on. Reports at the time suggested that the owner of the land, provided he was offered a big enough chunk of cash, was not against selling so that this could happen. However, the farmer leasing the land vehemently disagreed, citing the work his family, for generations, had carried out in order to turn the land into viable and effective farmland. So far nothing, it seemed, had happened.

Lying there in the thick of it, with no tent walls to remove it from me, and no barge to carry me across any mere, I was happy to be on now dry-ish land. But to allow some of the fens to thrive again, the great plains of water that we have worked our damndest over the last couple of hundred years to keep below the land may now need to be carefully re-wilded in order to preserve the very attractions people come here for.

I watched as the leaves to my left, where I'd heard the digging, rustled and seemed to move by themselves – either a badger or a mole was behind the movement, I was sure, or possibly a hedgehog. I wondered, as I gazed beyond the tree branches that seemed to stretch up to heaven itself, whether it would be worth bringing out some of the farmers to this land and making them spend a night within it to really appreciate the wildlife who live here and call it home – to prove that they really are worth saving.

At some point, while philosophising over that, I fell asleep, surrounded by life on all points of the compass. It was funny, this had been the 'lowest sleep' in terms of elevation, but all things considered, despite the fast food now gurgling in by belly, I felt pretty high.

Gunshot woke me with a start, later than I'd planned, and as I moved I sent the beads of water on the outside of my bivvy bag shooting off down the sides. Almost immediately after the gunshot had sounded, echoing in the morning sky, it was followed by squawks from geese, flapping overhead and noisily coming in to land somewhere nearby. Around me the forest continued to move and to breathe, itself alive with life of every sort. I'm still not sure precisely what was being shot at that day, but as long as it wasn't me I was happy. I took out my stove and began to brew up some hot water for a coffee. As it bubbled, I shook out my belongings and shoved them into my rucksack, remembering to do a short section to camera again before I did so.

Everything about me seemed damp; my kit, my hair, the camera, which I had a lot of difficulty even turning on. I supped my drink, shoving all my belongings into the bin bag by my rucksack and, as the sound of the plastic crinkling subsided, I just allowed myself to be at one with the forest.

A car shattered my private, silent reverie a few minutes later, breaking the hushed silence with its engine. Soon the dog-walkers would be out in full force and the car-parking spaces that now lay empty would likely fill up. As I sat there I thought about Ben Nevis once more and in particular about how a sleep at its summit had eluded me. By now I was on track to finish my Extreme Sleeps Challenge, with only that and my southernmost sleep left on the tick list.

The morning light was starting to break as the mist hung low at my ankles. I would need to nip into work on Monday, tomorrow, but technically the challenge could still be done. I'd managed five of my seven extreme sleeps, having completed the westernmost, northernmost, easternmost, most central and now the lowest point on mainland Britain. I had two sleeps left, and two days – or rather nights – to complete my challenge. But where to go next? I wasn't sure. I was tempted to linger here in Huntingdonshire, to soak in all the delights of a breaking dawn, knowing another sleep had been achieved. But success was within my grasp. All was not lost. I could still do this... couldn't I?

CHAPTER TWELVE

BEN, AGAIN

With time running out and work responsibilities beckoning down south, there was only one sensible thing to do – get as far away from them as possible. So now I turned my car north once more, setting a course from this, the lowest point in Britain, back to the highest – Ben Nevis – my penultimate camp in my Extreme Sleeps Challenge. And this time I was determined to do it right and see it through to the bitter end.

I always find it odd revisiting somewhere – especially a fairly wild place – that I've been to recently. At the end of my long drive north that afternoon, I dutifully restocked my supplies at the supermarket in Fort William, trying to ignore the fact that the top of The Ben was already, at this early stage, encased in a blanket of thick, grey cloud. When I headed down the valley once more, the same mix of dampening darkness I had experienced the last time seemed to greet me, though it was slightly earlier in the day, and my brain – as though a conditioned Pavlov's dog – seemed to wince at the muscle memory triggered of hiking up all the way to the top and then heaving back down two bags of leftover rubbish. Normally eager to get going once I reach a start point, at that particular one I had to force myself to get out of the car and restart on the path.

I had chosen the Pony Track again for its ease in route-finding and because of the clag that was refusing to budge from the top. I seemed to cover ground much quicker this time, though, feeling out the route in the grey mist with my feet, already innately knowing which way I should be heading, driven on by good, old-fashioned intuition.

Geologists theorise that this mountain was once an ancient volcano that became dormant around 350 million years ago after the dome-shaped summit collapsed in on itself one day, in what must have been one hell of a mighty big explosion (or implosion, even). Since then other traumas have helped shape it, from glaciers carving themselves through to man's determination to try to control it by cleaving footpaths into its flanks, constructing buildings and observation huts on its summit and maintaining the walkers' cairns that now line the footpath near to the summit trig point. It has been very heavily influenced in its design by both the natural and the man-made.

As I walked up its slopes now, enjoying the handily placed steps that have been created at the lower reaches (and are a complete knee-bugger on the way back down), I tried to imagine glowing crimson strips of lava boiling and glugging their way down the slopes, pulling up trees as they went, moving huge boulders along with them as though they were merely hundreds and thousands cake decorations being sprinkled on top of icing sugar, requiring no effort at all. I thought back to the implosion I had read about, the one that had created the hulking mass and shape of the mountain. Now with the thick grey cloud above, hanging around the top third of the summit, it looked like it had just happened. The mist resembled a plume of volcanic ash, the sky cast black by the falling debris, and yet I stood, unmoving, drinking in the drama as it engulfed and flowed around me.

As I reached Half Way Lochan I could just about make out the lights of Fort William. I looked below where I now stood, remembering my camp from several days previously. Though the weather higher up was going to be damp and undoubtedly windy, there was really no way I could abandon this attempt – it was make or break time.

I turned to continue uphill as the path cut right across the slopes. As with my last visit, sheep were noisily pacing the path ahead of me, making me feel like one of their herd. Even in the darkening light I could see their long, woolly tails bobbing along, a spray of their pellet droppings covering the path ahead.

From way down in Glen Nevis, where I had once again left my car, the mountain of Ben Nevis soars uphill in a rise of nearly 2 kilometres straight from the valley floor. It's a lot of climbing, with no other routes to really offer an alternative – unless you happen to be a rock climber or winter mountaineer, or very experienced and competent as a hillwalker. From my perspective, climbing to the top feels like you're conquering a sleeping beast, a great rising mass of bulk beckoning you to try your luck.

Today, I thought, as I stepped off the path for a second to see if I could peer down and get a clearer view of Five Finger Gully (so called because of the set of five chutes that cut down its sides), luck would not be in my favour. Above my head the dreary cloud continued to circle and build up tower-like, billowing and gaining momentum as it did so. As I stared down into the darkening valley at my feet, then up at the darkening peak above me, I felt the first drops of rainfall land with a tap upon my shoulder. I put on my waterproofs and continued onwards, wishing momentarily that the cloud would move off and I would be rewarded with views and warm sunshine.

I listened to the stones crack and crunch under the tread of my boots, some even seeming to pop with a satisfying rounded melody as I crushed them underfoot. Each step I took was slow and deliberate. Without realising my intention, I had made this attempt about taking my time to really get to grips with the mountain, to study it unrushed by weather or by my own agenda. Perhaps, I mused as I switched my direction on the zigzags, I was really doing it to delay the inevitable, the coming face to face with more rubbish, which I might feel determined to carry down once more.

Where the zigzags petered out into a more direct cutting of the path straight up, I was well and truly into the cloud. The wet rocks now below me were replaced by snow-plastered ones, the rain this high up falling as a mix of hail and snow. I cinched my hood cords so that it fitted flush to my face, bending the wire peak so that my cheeks were now bulging out the sides and reddening in the cold air.

Feeling myself sweat as I made the worst of the direct climbs, past the first marker cairn, I wondered what I would find on the summit. Another camper, perhaps? Not likely in this inclement weather, I corrected myself. Perhaps a rubbish-strewn summit that I would have to clean up again? Again, unlikely, I thought, as it couldn't have accumulated as much as I had had to carry down not even a week earlier.

Back in May 2006, workers for the charitable John Muir Trust came up here to find a piano that had been buried under a cairn on the summit. One of the theories is that it was carried up by a team of removal men from Dundee 20 years previously as part of a challenge they had set themselves to raise money, another is that it was actually a church organ carried up by Kenny Campbell, a woodcutter from Bonar Bridge. But in any event it wasn't the first time odd things had found their way to the top of the mountain. From an old motor car (in 1911 a Ford agent drove a Model T to the top as a publicity stunt) to a bed (Glasgow University students in 1981), and even a hotel (a Temperance one run in the summer months by two ladies between 1894 and 1916, it cost 10 shillings a night to stay there).

It seems odd that the highest peak in the UK has managed to be the receiver of these weird and wonderful spoils, but also remained naturally intact, without a cable car or railway station (both of which has been proposed at one time or another) on its summit.

As I reached the first bend of the swerve that makes up the kidney shape of the plateau, I could just about make out in the dimming light that the cornice – responsible for many an accident up here – had begun to form. As I looked at it the wind began to pick up – fast. A sudden gust sent a spray of snow across my face, picking it up from the ground and lashing it at me. I hunkered down, hunching my shoulders around my face for protection, all at once glad of the extra weight in my backpack. Being so near to the gully was quite a worry given the conditions and so, keeping my whole body to the ground, I edged towards the next marker cairn, which seemed to emerge from the gloom as a wonderfully man-made beacon of hope. My breathing had involuntarily quickened, and my senses had been heightened. As I neared the cairn, I worried that the next might not be as visible and so I braced myself for the prospect that I might need to take out my map and compass and get navigating. Just as I reached it, and had given up hope of seeing beyond, the next one began to appear, at first mirage-like, an unreal shape in the mist, but then with each step it became clearer.

The darkness was now becoming thick in the twilight and, though I knew I was nearly at the summit, I couldn't yet make out the shapes of the old observatory. Wind whistled on, seemingly funnelling up through the gullies that spread down from the summit like an intricate network of veins that had filled with rainwater or snow before freezing into icy flues. Of all the gullies here my particularly favourite – through its name alone – is one called Gardyloo. Don't get me wrong, I've never climbed it, but I love the history to it. Sitting as it does between Tower Ridge and Observatory Ridge, it was once used as trash chute for those stationed at the observatory tower. As such, it became nicknamed as *garde à l'eau* (obviously pronounced Gardyloo) gully, *garde à l'eau* being French for 'Watch out for the water', a common phrase in the days before sanitation in the streets of any major city, shouted as a warning to pedestrians below that slop was about to be flung from the window. Charming.

The wind was howling by the time I reached the first of the dilapidated buildings where the window arches are still, remarkably, intact. I had brought a tent with me and planned to pitch it somewhere in the lee of the ruins to offer some protection against the wind. I switched on my head torch. Looking around, I could only really see the rain bouncing off my beam and, beyond that, only the very tops of the crumbling brickwork.

I took off my rucksack and let it slouch against the war memorial I had seen many times before. Raising my arms up to the sky, I enjoyed the temporary enlightened feeling following the rucksack's removal. I turned a full 360 degrees to check out whom I would be sharing my summit with. At first I thought I saw movement near the trig point, but it revealed itself to be nothing more than a bird. Then I looked over towards the emergency shelter, its doors shut tight against the elements.

I grabbed my tent and headed for what appeared to be some flattened land among the buildings. When I got there, my foot slipped on what was actually revealed to be a series of fallen stones covered with snow and made slick from meltwater. Battling to stay upright, my hand was still in my walking-pole loop when I fell. My whole arm now tugged against the pole as it dug fast into the snow and stone. The pole yanked itself out from its position under my body weight and I landed hard on my wrist, my feet hurtling skyward.

I sat for a few seconds taking in my circumstances and wondering just what I would do next. With my wrist throbbing, I decided to crawl out from this space and instead make for some more exposed but definitely solid land around the trig point. Wincing each time I had to move my arm around, I pulled out my tarp groundsheet and set to work erecting the tent. All was going well until I tried to put the poles in and then a burst of wind came and lifted the fabric up and clean out of my hands. Bounding across the plateau like an overexcited sheepdog, I jumped and leapt over obstacles as though indulging in some high-altitude parcour. I knew I'd soon reach the edge of the cliffs, so I dived for the fabric and landed hard on the ground. As I went down I heard one of the loudest, scariest sounds I have ever heard in all my years of camping – my tent had ripped.

My friend works as an outdoor-gear tester and I'll never forget him testing a whole bunch of two-man tent models for a comparative review in 2009. He was so thorough that he even sent sections of the waterproof outer sheet to scientists at Leeds University, who pressure-tested and waterproof-tested them in controlled lab conditions so that he could be sure that any claims he made about their abilities to stand up to a storm, remain durable on rocky ground and survive the rigours of a windy night came from him and not the marketing department of the outdoor-gear company. It was a great plan and showed unwavering integrity in the face of advertising pressure. It did, however, prove a problem when, months after said tests, he lent a bunch of us different tents to try out, but neglected to remember that some were from that particular sample. That of course meant that when we reached our wonderful wild-camping spots in the middle of the mountains and erected our prizes, many of us were shocked to find that our walls were riddled with an abundance of large holes in the side or the roof – not ideal as rain was on the horizon. Needless to say, we had to abandon our much-longed-for campsite and relegate it for another day's adventure. If I felt bad back then, now I felt ten times worse. With no companions to comfort me, I swallowed hard, trying to keep it together.

Standing up, I pulled the tent in front of me, expecting to see a tear similar to the great hole of 2009. Instead, after a quick search, it revealed itself to be nothing more than a 5-centimetre line-tear between the inbuilt groundsheet and the sides of the wall. It was ripstop fabric and had showed its durability admirably. I was both annoyed and relieved.

I didn't have time to contemplate my next move very thoroughly. Almost as quickly as I had located the casualty on the tent, another squall of wind tried to pinch it from my grasp once more. If I was going to stay here, it had become immediately clear to me that I would need to sleep inside the emergency shelter, aka the world's highest fridge you can sleep inside.

I did momentarily think that it might be better to leave the summit altogether, on account of that being safer than lingering on Britain's highest spot in increasingly unpredictable gale-force winds. I bundled my tent together and ran over to where I had left my bag. Without stopping to even check if I'd left anything behind, I collected everything up and made for the steps to the shelter, each one coated in a thick patch of snow.

I opened the heavy metal bolt and let the door swing open. Inside there was no one silly enough to be here on this especially windy evening. I crawled inside, turned my head torch up to its full-beam setting and looked into each of the four corners. Now I couldn't help but smile. There was no rubbish, not even any tissues, to be found. I couldn't help but feel that I had somehow contributed to this state of affairs by removing all that rubbish the week before. I had perhaps stopped other people from being blasé about it and adding their personal collections to any new mound. I sat for a good minute looking around the rubbish-free wooden shelter, a huge smile plastered to my face. 'This was worth coming back for,' I said out loud as I shivered in the cold.

Though this hut is definitely the highest one in Britain – the roof of the building is even higher than the trig point itself – it's certainly not the only man-made shelter on the mountain. In 1929 the Scottish Mountaineering Club's CIC hut (CIC standing for Charles Inglis Clark, who instigated a number of new routes on The Ben in his prime) was built in Coire Leis, at a spot height of around 600 metres beneath the north face of the mountain. Sadly, unlike this emergency shelter I was currently freezing inside, it is privately owned and is for use by the club's members only.

Now in my own little shelter, with the wind rattling outside, I felt a little normality return. I could think straight and go through my kit properly. I pulled out an extra mid-layer I had brought and span it so that I could tie the two arms together to use it as a makeshift sling to take the pressure off my sore wrist. Once that was done, I set to work trying to make this place as homely as possible. Having thought at the outset that it might be a possibility that I would have to sleep inside it, on account of the particularly bad weather, I had come along well prepared. As well as my tent, which I now needed to unravel from the spaghetti junction of guy lines and bungee cords that had become dislodged outside, I had remembered to bring with me a bivvy bag, as I knew how damp this place can get. In addition, I had brought extra snack food in the form of my favourite chocolate and cereal bars, and even a spare bottle to make into a hot water bottle to keep me warm. The worst thing was that it wasn't even that late yet, just a little after 9 p.m., but the darkness outside was complete.

It was hard to believe that with this kind of weather – which comes with amazing regularity in this high place – The Ben had become such a Mecca for climbing in both the summer and the winter. In the first half of the twentieth century many people had put up first ascents on the rocks that led to the summit, but even as recently as 2008 a climber put up a new ungraded climb – after an impressive two years of planning. The Ben, it seems, is forever throwing up new surprises for people.

Thankfully, sleeping doesn't take as much time to plan and it wasn't long before I was bundled up in my sleeping bag, which itself was safely stashed inside the protection of a waterproof bivvy. My stove was on, boiling up my meal, and I was wrapped up in a layered mix of merino wool, fleece, a waterproof and insulated jacket, a big thick woolly hat, some gloves (both liners and down-filled outer mittens), two pairs of socks and woollen long johns under my lined walking trousers – and still I was cold. No matter what I did to try and counter it, there was no escaping the fact that this wooden box, perched high on a little ramshackle tower of rock, was for emergency use only.

The steam from my stove filled the air immediately, forging a massive white steam cloud. I was instantly blind to my surrounds, and fumbled across the wooden platform to reach the door. Locating the bolt, I opened the door wide to allow the steam to escape. Almost as soon as I did so, the chill of cold damp air blasted inside and the steam was stolen on the breeze, sucked out of the hut with barely any effort required. I was forced to leave it open the whole time I cooked, not wanted to risk getting engulfed again in cloud. Even once the meal was ready for eating, it didn't end there. The steam from my meal itself – which wasn't even particularly hot by the time I was ready for eating it – filled the tiny space quickly and I was once more forced to shimmy over to what I affectionately dubbed the freezer door to let it escape.

By the time my meal was over the whole place seemed to be dripping with water. Beads of condensation gathered and fell above me and down the side walls too, meaning I couldn't even rest against them. The sleeping mat that had been left up here when I'd visited a week ago was still here now, but was still as wet as ever, so I'd opted not to use it. Instead, I gathered it up and folded it into the draughtiest corner, hoping it would save me from getting wet.

The air was thick with a bitter cold. Above me I watched as another droplet of water, condensed in the relative warmth of my shelter, collected itself and trickled along the roof-supporting metal piping. It travelled down the tubing for a couple of seconds before hanging in an elongated pause, above where I was lying. I watched it intently, willing it to fall and end the suspense, but at the same time wondering if I could make it disappear and roll instead down to the wall and then hit the floor with a splash away from me. I kept my eyes on it, wondering if this suspended animation would ever pass, but nothing happened and still I waited.

I looked about me. This little wooden box was dark and still. Wrapped up inside the confines of my sleeping bag, which boasted an extreme rating of −32°C, I still felt my body shake with the cold. From my numb toes right up to the tips of my fingers, only my breath seemed warmer, casting in the darkness a murky cloud of warm air every few seconds as I exhaled.

PLUIP! The droplet of water had finally left its high point and fallen with a very loud plop, right onto me. When I'd arrived at the safety of the shelter earlier, it had seemed like the perfect salvation in a storm. Now, however, I felt like I was sleeping inside a refrigerator, the big metal closure system on the door shut tight, every corner of the space cold and shut off from the light.

Rather than the warm, dry space you'd expect to get inside a mountain bothy, it seemed to generate coldness from every angle. As the hours passed by, I began my never-ending battle to make hot water for tea, in between shuffling over to the door to fling it open to release the condensation. When I got bored of that one, I started playing the merry game of 'move out of the way of the dropping water', making bets with myself over which bead would be the first to rain down on me – with bonus points available if I could guess which body part it would hit. I never once felt myself warm up. The space is too small to stand up in, so the best movement is done on all fours, or not at all, which is what I opted for.

I had wanted this high sleep to be a triumphant moment, but so far all I seemed to be doing was checking the clock every 10 minutes, waiting and hoping for morning so I could claim my prize of having established a camp of sorts here and head back down. Then I remembered the whisky.

Down beneath the foot of Ben Nevis sits a distillery that creates single-malt delights, using none other than the water from the Allt a'Mhuilinn river, which makes its way down via the northern corries of the mountain. Founded as it was in

1825, it is one of the oldest licensed distilleries in Scotland. And before I had left the glen earlier that same evening, I had managed to locate some – so that I could raise a glass to the mountain in celebration if I finally managed to do this sleep.

I went through my food bag and found my little hip flask. Without waiting for a cup (I didn't really have one) I gulped greedily from the bottle, the warm amber liquid soothing my throat as I drank. As I swallowed, I could feel the whisky spreading in my chest, creating a burning cavity in the centre. For the first time that evening I began to feel quite warm.

I'd read of people staying the night here before, often rudely awakened by walkers out late or early, who had 'just stopped by for a look'. Tonight, though, in this mini-storm, with the wind whipping the snow outside back up into the air – re-snowing, if you will – I was the only one crazy enough to be out in it. I wished I had battery left in the video camera, wished I had a way to charge it to record my thoughts. It had died somewhere along the way, after my attempts to film sections on the way up, but only managing to capture short bursts of footage before it turned itself off again. But then, not having it had in some respects allowed me to go back to basics and have some time to reflect on the mountain on which I found myself on my penultimate extreme sleep in this self-prescribed challenge.

I was glad I had chosen sleeping as my primary 'theme', because it had allowed me thinking time, not only to look at and think about where I was going, but also to look back at where I had been. This was much better than the alternative of dashing around like a lunatic, so typical of other people who undertake these kinds of challenges with little or no appreciation of their surrounds.

I thought back to the fell runners I'd seen on all of the mountains I'd been on, who in one respect seemed to have it really good, in the sense that they can get out there in the mountains unencumbered by the piles of modern kit designed to make us more comfortable and more lightweight. In other words, they can just enjoy it. On the other hand, though, for them it really is about hitting the summit and then turning around to make it back – they too have no time allowed to take in the views.

Of course running on The Ben is nothing new. Back as early as 1895 there were people keen to hold the record for the timed ascent up the mountain and descent back into town. It all started with a barber called William Swan, who in September that year ran up the mountain and back down again in 2 hours 41 minutes – a quick bit of maths and I realised that he'd manage to ascend and descend Britain's highest mountain in under the time it had taken me to drive from Glasgow up to Fort William. Following that, of course, things became competitive, with many people trying to beat his time. Many did, and it became an annual event, being a race that continues to be run every September to this day. Although it suffered a hiatus following the closure of the observatory at the summit, since 1937 the Ben Nevis Race has seen up to 600 people running from the football grounds on the outskirts of town up to the summit and back. So tough is this mountain race that you are turned back if the summit has not been reached within your first 2 hours of running. The race record stands at just 1 hour 25 minutes, held since 1984 by Englishman Kenny Stuart. Remarkably, his wife Pauline set the women's record of 1 hour 43 minutes that same year.

Knowing I wouldn't sleep in such a cold cabin, I lay awake in my sleeping bag wondering if anyone would see my extreme sleeps as a record to beat. I lay there shivering, watching more water gather on the ceiling above me, knowing that any minute now it would begin cascading down onto me. Then I got tired of waiting and banged the wall with my feet. I watched as a gush of water began falling on me from above, and I laughed.

Somehow between the dripping water and the sub-zero temperatures, and several more swigs of whisky, I eventually dropped off to sleep, waking only a couple of times to find that part of my body had become so numb that I was forced to turn over to my other side. I drifted in and out of my deep-freeze slumber and somehow avoided falling off the tiny raised sleeping platform.

When I woke for the third time and checked my clock, I was surprised to see that it was close to 6 a.m. I was still cold and I breathed a sigh at the thought of getting out of my relatively warm layers of sleeping bag and bivvy to emerge into the dim morning light that would be waiting outside. I stretched out my arms in a yawn and felt the tug of the sling I had left on. To my relief, my wrist seemed less painful; it must have only been a light sprain.

And so, somewhere up in the clouds, I drank a hot drink while perched on the edge of the steps of the survival shelter, the highest person in Britain to be having their breakfast. And the first woman to complete the 3 Peaks Sleeps Challenge. The novelty was palpable.

I didn't get the views that morning that I had enjoyed on my last visit. There were no island-like mountaintops peeking through the clouds, no sunshine on my face or sunsets to defy all sunsets, but there was no rubbish either, and that knowledge made each step down all the sweeter. At Half Way Lochan my phone beeped again and to my delight I saw that someone had posted that they'd just been up to their local hill and filled a bag of rubbish and taken it down, inspired by my actions on Ben Nevis earlier that week. I had to stop myself from crying joyfully. Even if no one ever tried to mimic my sleeping antics, it didn't matter; if I could get a few more people to follow in my footsteps and remove rubbish from a beautiful wild place, then my work was definitely done.

And just then it occurred to me – I had nearly done it. My Extreme Sleeps Challenge was almost complete. With The Ben under my belt, I had just one sleep left – the most southerly, at Lizard Point, way down on the Cornish coast. All that separated me from it was a little over 600 miles and about 12 hours of driving – plus, I needed to call into work on the way. With that thought, I quickened my pace and didn't slow down all the way to the car.

CHAPTER THIRTEEN

LIZARD POINT

All the best stories start around midnight and this tale of the point at which I finished my Extreme Sleeps Challenge – and thereby all my self-set challenges – is no exception. There's something quite magical about this time of the evening, the moment when all the clock hands line up perfectly, when the chimes make the most noise for the most sustained period of time and when, in our imaginations, anything could happen – from secret gardens being exposed to ghosts appearing as apparitions.

At this particular midnight, on a cold December Monday evening, I was walking along the coastline from the rocky inlets of Kynance Cove on a very determined journey to the south-east, to spend the night on the southernmost point of mainland Britain – Lizard Point.

Much like poor Dunnet Head misses out on the headlines to its more easterly neighbour of John o'Groats, Lizard Point is the victim of a scene-stealing more westerly neighbour. Ask many people if they've stood on the southernmost point of

Britain and they will probably tell you, 'Yes – I've been to Land's End'. But much like its northerly counterpart of John o'Groats, Land's End is also a fraud, a tourist trap only, and not the southernmost point on the British mainland by some miles.

Set south from the little village of Lizard, the little peninsula of land known as Lizard Point juts out into the English Channel at a bearing of 49° 57' 30" N, making it the southernmost tip of mainland Britain. This wasn't my first time coming to this place for a sleep, though it was the first time I was planning to sleep right out at the edge of it. I'd first come to it many years before when I made my transition from mattress lover to wild camper.

I remember back then I had singled it out for the same reason I had done now – it was the most southerly point of mainland Britain and therefore the perfect place for me to begin an adventure that would take me all over the UK in a quest to fall back in love with the country, my country, that I had been neglecting in the name of travel. It was a time when I truly believed that Adventure (with a capital A) was something that lurked in far and distant lands, rather than right here in my own backyard. I had begun there and then to make my way up the country sleeping in caves, on mountain summits, under boulders and in bothies, becoming more wise to the wonderfully wild offerings Britain had going for it, and reigniting my love affair with the country I call home. That was where my love for wild nights had begun, and so it seemed a fitting ending to be there now on the final night of my challenge.

Unlike last time I visited – when I mistakenly brought a large tent with dayglo guy lines that lit up like Christmas tree lights every time the lighthouse beam shot round past me – this time I had only brought with me my bivvy bag, small, discreet and coloured dark green and black, perfect for bedding down above the high cliffs of this beautifully rugged coastline.

I nearly didn't make it at all – the whole challenge had been nearly scuppered. Because I had needed to go back up north to Ben Nevis to properly sleep on its summit, that had meant getting up and off the mountain a little after 6 a.m. as soon as I had enjoyed my coffee and biscuits. Practically sprinting off the peak, I had given all those fell runners a (pardon the pun) run for their money in the timing stakes. I had leapt into my car and bombed it down south in time to nip into work for the remainder of the day. With no days off left to take and a weekend now five nights away, I had left myself only one option – to do my final sleep on a work night, after I'd finished with my responsibilities for the day, kip on the cliffs, and then race back the next morning for a slightly later than normal start.

It was risky and it had meant an incredibly long day, but what it also meant was that I would definitely sleep well, tired out by a combination of a full-on work day as well as a hell of a lot of driving.

When I'd left the office, I had grabbed a handful of Clif Bars off my desk. I was the first to leave, like a child leaving school at the sound of the home-time bell. I started heading south but I was weary as soon as I hit the road. With my Go Bag in tow, though, I began to feel the adrenaline pumping through my veins once more, along with the excitement I always feel when heading out on a wild sleep. Knowing I would complete my challenge also added an extra dimension to my excitement level, so by the time I reached the turn-off for the peninsula I was practically giddy with anticipation.

Last time I had come here I had parked my car in the village of Lizard itself and treated myself to a hot pub meal before heading first to the southernmost point then veering west to find a more secluded spot away from the open elements. This time I would be doing the complete opposite. Instead of Lizard I parked above Kynance Cove and left my car there, ready to head to the blatant non-campsite at Lizard Point itself. I would just be lying there in the open for all to see – well, those that thought to look and see I was there anyway.

I made my way across the headland, following the path as it rose and fell above the waves crashing below. I decided to stop and do a bit to camera, the conclusion to my adventure. Reaching inside my rucksack I realised with a sinking feeling in my stomach that the camera bag was not properly zipped. Thinking back to my rush to leave the office, I could now, as I felt around frantically for it, picture it sitting there, safely charging while plugged in under my desk. I cursed myself for this oversight. There was no point getting upset, though. I would have to do my final footage using my phone. I stood fuming for a minute but then I heard the water froth and fizz as it always does in the evening, and despite the darkness I could make out the white rollers curling just metres below my feet. This was the reason I was here, to finish what I'd started, so I began to walk on.

For sailors Lizard Point is often the jumping-off point for adventure, and as such it is surprisingly busy. As I walked, I could make out the lights of the many ships that cruised along past each other, heading west or east, their lights twinkling in the night sky.

Another claim to fame for this stretch of coast is that in 1588, at 3 p.m. on 29 July to be precise, the ships that made up the mighty Spanish Armada were first spotted from Lizard Point. Consisting of 120 ships, it must have been one incredibly scary sight to behold. I stopped for a second now on the cliffs above Pistol Meadow and imagined what that person must have felt when the huge battalion of armed sailors, complete with cannons, was coming straight at them. Despite my warm jacket, I shivered.

With each step I was getting closer to Lizard village, which from here was lit up like the ships. The houses beyond the fields to my left glowed with an inviting yellow warmth in this supercilious December evening, the first day of the last month of the year. Above them the beam from the tall stone lighthouse swung around in a constant rhythm. That had been a common sight on this trip, the constant form of reassuring light at each of the country's compass points emanating from a little lighthouse from days gone by.

The one at Lizard is particularly special. Built in 1751, it had been much fought for after many a ship had been downed by the deadly offshore knot of underwater stones known as the Man o'War Rocks. These had seemingly been designed with the mission of slicing open the side of a metal ship as easily as a can opener cuts through an aluminium tin. There were many shipwrecks before the lighthouse was installed, with one in particular being more memorable than the others. The *Royal Anne Galley* saw the 15 souls aboard lose their lives when it smashed against one of the cliffs during the unrelenting tides of a nasty storm. All those lost were buried en masse in the meadowland which I was now walking through, the long grass surrounding my ankles like outstretched bony arms. It was a sad end for the seamen and their families, but in a strange twist of nature, this same field is now a place where Cornish chough choose to come to breed, starting new life in a place where goodbye was said to others.

I paused for a moment among the tree branches. It's somewhat ironic that at this part of the coast the beam from the lighthouse is least visible – unlike on the approach where you can't help but become blinded by it. In the past, when I first started out solo wild camping I would have been spooked to stand alone in such a place, associated as it is with death and ghost stories. But now, years on, I am happy to linger, feeling a sense of peace rather than dread, feeling comforted by any presence felt rather than warned off by it.

Even after the lighthouse was completed it didn't mean that all ships avoided the perils that lurked below the waves. As recently as 2004 a French trawler called *Bugaled Breizh* sank just off Lizard Point, resulting in the deaths of five crewmen. The place can be treacherous even today.

Twigs snapped loudly under my feet as I set off again, popping under the pressure as though mini-explosions at my boots. I continued on to Lizard Point, cutting first beneath the houses on the edge of Britain and then down and past the array of gift shops that line the final point. Here, despite signs advising otherwise, were several cars parked, each one looking grey in the evening light. A few metres beyond them was a small patch of grass and beyond that still were the edges of the cliffs which dropped down to sea at the southernmost point of the mainland.

I walked down to near to the edge as I would dare and felt the wind push me back as waves hammered at the rocks below. There was nothing else for it, this was where I had to make camp for the night, here was where I needed to complete my Extreme Sleeps Challenge.

I undid my bag and pulled out my bivvy, already set up with my sleeping bag and liner inside. Much like how I did on the slopes of Dunnet Head, here I planned to anchor myself down so that I couldn't plunge below during my sleep only to be swallowed up by the shadowy waves and taken out to sea.

I removed my waterproof and instead snuggled into my warm duvet jacket, rammed full of insulation. I'd brought a foam mat to place underneath me and I perched my boots above me, their laces wet from the grass I had passed through to make it here. Careful not to roll as I wiggled further into my bag and bivvy, I felt my feet momentarily balance over nothing at all and quickly corrected myself by shuffling backwards to the safety of the land. Tying myself loosely to a nearby rock I was somewhat secure, but vowed to keep myself as still as possible.

With one last look behind me to check I was still alone, I pushed my bag right down so that it wouldn't be visible by anyone on the approach and then lay my head down too, so that I would be hidden from view also.

Once more the sounds of the sea were deafening and all at once it took me back to my very first wild sleep down here, where the crescendo of waves and calling birds combined with the spinning lighthouse beam had made it impossible to sleep. Now, however, despite the noise I found myself being lulled slowly, dreaming of shipwrecks and big surf, awoken only a couple of times by the passing spray of the briny water, carried far on the wind of this cool early winter's evening.

It had been on an evening in the late winter of 1907 when this bay became alive with the busy sounds off an RNLI lifeboat rescue in full swing. It was mid March and the SS *Suevic*, caught up in the midst of a windstorm and blinded by a film of thick fog, hit the rocky reef that lies just south of the point. Unlike with the *Royal Anne Galley*, the results were somewhat happier. Volunteers from Lizard RNLI station, as well as three other Cornish stations, worked tirelessly throughout the night and managed to rescue 456 passengers, including, it is said, around 70 babies, all in a period of 16 hours. Proof that when we humans are put to the test, when we are pushed to the absolute limit, when we're so cold and tired that we feel we can't go on any further, we really do manage to show what we are truly capable of.

I lay there now, breathing in the delicious salt of the sea air, the spray in my face and droplets lingering in my hair, and I felt glad that it was to be the final place on my journey – a place where the landscape did as it pleased (the cliffs there are constantly collapsing of their own accord, and the walking paths often need to be diverted) and people worked hard to live life on the edge, never afraid to help out others in need.

It's said that a little further along the coast at Kennack Sands near Cadgwith, a swashbuckling pirate called Henry Avery buried some of his treasure, leaving the rest hidden at nearby Gunwalloe. Locals will also tell you the tale of two sunken ships that are known to have been carrying treasure, and which were brought down near Church Cove in the years 1526 and 1785 respectively. Many have tried – and failed – to find the legendary gold and precious metals they were said to have been carrying, but then perhaps, as with Merlin's throne on Snowdon, the treasure of exploring these coves goes deeper than riches in the monetary sense.

I turned over in my sleeping bag, turning now to face the earth, its damp, grassy texture brushing up against my nose, the moist scent of soil smelling good and wholesome in my nostrils, and I closed my eyes again.

I woke a little later upon hearing the slamming of car doors somewhere above where I lay. I froze instinctively, fighting the urge to sit up. Like a child I kept my eyes closed; my logic being that if I couldn't see them then they couldn't see me. Seconds later I could make out the sound of a vehicle powering up and the driver speeding off.

I exhaled loudly, glad they had gone. Aching a little from my previous position, my back cold from the constant cool breeze that had found its way inside my sleeping bag, I turned to face the waves once more. It was funny to think that from this point I could get a boat, set sail for the south and head off on a watery adventure without a single person – myself included – knowing where I might end up.

This challenge I had set myself had embraced elements of the unknown, like the weather that had forced me to turn back on Ben Nevis and sleep much lower down, and the urban circumstances that had caused me to sleep burrowed like a rabbit amid the discarded clothes of a romantic fumble alongside a septic interceptor on the easternmost reaches of England. But I had known all along that I would end up here at Lizard Point. I didn't know where I would head to after this, beyond going back to work and my daily rituals and responsibilities on the magazine, but I knew that my adventures would take me somewhere. Like the beam of the lighthouse torch stretching out overhead, I knew I still had some distance to cover, even though I wasn't sure yet where that distance would take me. Once more I drifted off, like the great ocean waves, sleep washing over me in a welcome surge.

My head was still full of buccaneers and smugglers. Before coming back to Lizard Point I had been reading more tales of the lawbreaking rebels who would use the nooks and crannies of the coastline to hide their illegal wares (mainly drink), to sell on to locals. Owing to the tales of battles involving these shady characters, ghost stories abound, with many a phantom ship spied from the shore. In fact, author Daphne du Maurier based a lot of her swaggering, romantic tales on the landscapes here, and on stories she heard in this part of the world.

A giant wave crashed below, its echo reverberating up the cliff-side where I lay and I swear the whole thing shook violently. I immediately jolted upright this time, disturbed. My bivvy bag was wet from head to toe with the blast, the gusting wind now picking up into something more closely resembling a squall. I wriggled out of my wet bag and, shakily, got to my feet, my legs weak after hours spent stationary. I checked the time. I had 10 minutes left until it was 6.30 a.m. I had nearly made it.

Shaking off the bivvy bag, I climbed reluctantly back inside it, now eager to be heading back to my car, where at least I would be dry. I knew I wouldn't go back to sleep in these final few minutes, so instead I lay down with my eyes wide open, taking in this, my last sleep of the challenge, with every sense alert.

It was still dark out there, the horizon defined by the number of ships still illuminated in the darkness by their internal lighting. Above, the circuit of the lighthouse beam continued on her predictable course. My fingertips felt cold and hard, my head ached from where I had slept funny on my hairline, pressing it the wrong way for too many hours. The combined scent of salt and seaweed was overpowering in my nose, making me feel as though any minute I might begin a torrent of sneezing. In the wind, my eyes began to stream with brackish tears, and my head was full of the sounds of that same shrill, yowling wind circling around my head and the thunderous roar of the waves, now crashing a little further out below.

I didn't hear my alarm when it went off to alert me that the time had gone by, such was the din of nature there. But minutes later I moved, sensing that my time had come to leave, and I began to pack up my belongings.

Feeling slightly dishevelled, I pulled my rucksack onto my back and looked around me for signs of life. At 6.35 a.m. it was distinctly quiet. Being a Tuesday morning, people were clearly still in bed or at least preparing for the working day ahead of them. Nowadays the south-west coast is a collection of sleepy villages and coastal hubs of local shops and chippies, seemingly designed to get us away from invasive technology and the hubbub of the cities.

As I began to head back to Kynance, treading the South West Coast Path, I peered into the dimly lit window of the gift shop here at Lizard Point to see the spoils on offer. From shells and plaques depicting Lizard Point to sticks of rock, it seemed all the usual paraphernalia could be bought here. One item caught my eye in particular – a funny sort of rock that seemed to be glowing a darkened shade of jade, with red and white layers running through it. This was the native serpentine stone of which the Lizard Point is made. Back when the coast was king, and hordes of Victorians would escape to the British seaside, little trinkets made from this novelty piece of geological formation were all the rage and villagers took up the trade of sculpting it to make money. Nowadays the souvenir business is not as big as it once was, and so far fewer bother with the craft.

I continued past this and climbed up the grassy banks below some blue-and-white houses, on which life rings provided the nautical decoration and carvings of powder-blue lighthouses added a splash of pastel to the scene. The wind blew at my face, helping me to wake in the early morning.

I needed to rush to get back to work, to hit the road before the traffic gathered with noisy and impatient commuters, but it was difficult to make myself do anything more than a steady pace, reluctant to give up my little shoreline stroll to be confined in the four metal walls of my vehicle. Above, the seagulls cawed for attention, floating on the breeze, and kittiwakes joined the crowd, all heralding a new morning here by the sea. I lingered just a few minutes, taking in the sounds that would, just hours later, be replaced by the chatter of co-workers talking in the office, the sound of printers cluttering busily away, the steady Xeroxing of papers and the tap-tap of keyboards being worked on by eager, lively fingers.

I passed a sign that advised of a detour due to landslide, a detour I hadn't noticed on my way here, having been too focused on reaching my goal in the evening light. I continued on, feeling the grassy ground spring beneath my feet as I went, and inhaled the air deeply, the sea air a curative for my usual office oxygen.

Soon I reached the familiar sight of Kynance Cove, where I'd started out from the previous night, and where my adventure would come to an end. I felt strange. On the one hand, I was elated and enthralled that I had set myself a challenge and successfully completed it, despite having to overcome a fair number of obstacles along the way. But, on the other hand, I felt the low ebb that every adventurer feels when the goal has been achieved – a slight feeling of emptiness, knowing that you've come to the end of a road and that the adventure is over.

I delayed the inevitable, not yet getting into the car, not wanting to admit that this was finished and that life must now go on, back to normal. It wasn't like when I had finished my last British adventure, having ended in glorious fashion on the white silt of Sandwood Bay in north-west Scotland, having renewed my love for the country I call home. This time I had already loved it when I started out. I had set myself three challenges: to sleep in the remotest places in Scotland; to sleep at the highest points of England, Scotland and Wales, and to bed down at the extremes of mainland Britain. In doing so, I had sought to find the ultimate place to wild camp. I had wanted to undertake a proper time-intensive challenge, a committed series of nights under canvas, ot at least in my bivvy, to see if it would make me connect with the landscapes in a deeper way and to discover if it would change me in any way.

The truth was I had changed – but not in the way I had anticipated. I had come to realise that these self-set challenges, these endless pursuits of being the first/youngest/oldest to do something, aren't arbitrary and pointless. Claiming the accolade itself might be – I still believed that – but setting a goal and sticking to it, seeing it through while battling with hardships and scary moments, made you not only push yourself further, but also made you want to be a better person. Whether that meant picking up litter that someone else had dropped in a wild place to make that place more pleasant for others, or helping someone dry out after they've just had a traumatic experience crossing a river in spate, or simply reflecting on how your own actions, no matter how small, can have an impact on other people, and possibly even inspire them to be better people too.

Setting myself these challenges initially to show someone else (Middle-Aged Man in Lycra) not to be so closed-minded had opened my own mind too. Had it not been for these challenges, had I never aimed to seek out the 'true' extremes of Britain, I would never have found places like Ardnamurchan, never have taken the time to linger on Snowdon, a mountain I had relegated as one for the tourists, and never truly appreciated the pockets of wilderness you can get in the urban world, like those I found in Lowestoft.

I stood looking out to sea and down to the cove, and then off in the direction where I knew my car, my route back to civilisation and the end of my three challenges waited. They say that hidden in the rocks here at Kynance, below where I was now rooted to the spot, there is a network of labyrinthine interconnected caves that are perfect for exploring at low tide. The idea excited and scared me in equal measure. I walked away slowly, imagining being in a place where any minute a turn could mean the difference between an opening onto a picture-perfect beach or an avenue into multiple unknown possibilities, a doorway into other doorways, where tunnels upon tunnels await, each one offering the excitement of the unknown, each one promising the thrill of adventure.

****

On 2 December 2014 Phoebe Smith became the first woman to have slept at all of mainland Britain's extremities. She also became the first person to have slept at all the extremities plus the centremost point of Britain on consecutive nights.

AFTER THE CHALLENGE

My tent door framed the view perfectly, the line of the zip creating a suitably jagged black border. The sand stretched on outside, past my boots, which were stained practically pink by the setting sun. The light reflected on the surface water so brightly that it seemed to vanish into the light, glowing almost white. The backdrop was formed of the mountainous isles of Skye, Rum and Eigg, and dappled across the ground near my feet were pieces of green and black seaweed, adding a splash of colour as though thoughtfully placed, like light on a watercolour masterpiece.

If you'd have asked me to paint a picture of a perfect pitch, then this would be it – and the fact that getting here took a lot of effort made it even more special.

I was in Knoydart, up in the north-western reaches of Scotland. After I'd completed my Extreme Sleeps Challenge, I had headed dutifully back to work, arriving late that Tuesday morning. Someone told me that, in completing my challenge, I had become the first woman to sleep on all of Britain's extremities on consecutive nights, and the first person to do so including the centremost point of the UK. It was great to know, but the title didn't leave me feeling special – though the experience did.

Life had continued, responsibilities had piled on and I had once more found myself asking – what next? I needed to give myself something else to do that didn't involve timings or extremities but instead just allowed me to do something that I had wanted to do for a while. So I took a long weekend and headed north all the way up to Mallaig, the rail terminal of the scenic West Highland Line from Oban, the same line that the Hogwarts Express uses to deliver Harry Potter and his fellow pupils to school. Among the cafes and chippies is the most important part of the town – its harbour. It's a place where ferries travel back and forward to the isles of Skye, Eigg and Rum, and it's where I managed to blag a ride on a boat to Barrisdale on the Knoydart Peninsula.

The adventure had started quickly. I had just enough time to run and pick up my bag from the car once I'd secured the ride, but no time to purchase any food. I stared at the horizon as the small sailboat I'd 'stowed away' on cranked up its engine, bound for a cluster of rocks that jut out from the beach at Barrisdale Bay.

'We won't be able to get in too close today as its low tide,' shouted one of the sail hands. 'You might need to make a jump for it and it will be a little bit of a scramble too,' he advised as the large stony protrusions appeared to our right.

A leap and a scramble, this was already becoming a bit more of an adventure than I had thought it was going to be. We got as close to them as we could and then he gestured for me to climb up onto the side of the boat. I did so, and then suddenly took a leap over the gap between my floating platform and the land, a gap which widened as I jumped. I landed fairly ungracefully, but I was instantly elated. I had made it onto Knoydart Peninsula – aka Scotland's Last Great Wilderness.

While it's true that, if you were to type 'Last Great Wilderness' into a well-known internet search engine, you would be presented with a huge range of options, several of which would be within Scotland, the peninsula upon which I had just so elegantly landed does lay claim to the title with good reason.

Jutting out into the water, splicing the two lochs of Nevis and Hourn with its mountainous interior, it is an area where the residents number just 100 during the summer, and less during the winter – in fact, it's one of the few places in the UK where you can safely say that the number of wild deer outnumber the humans. As for what might pass as a town, there is a small hamlet called Inverie, made up of a handful of houses and a single road that stretches along for about 7 miles and is not connected to the rest of the UK mainland road network. Getting here is by two ways and two ways only – by boat or on foot – or a combination of the two.

Boats normally drop you in Inverie itself, at a harbour near the pub – The Old Forge – which is officially the most remote pub in mainland Britain and the reason for many a visit, but my boat, the little sailing vessel I had managed to hitch a ride on, was different.

Nestled at the foot of a chain of bristly peaks is a collection of buildings called Barisdale, just about a mile up from Barrisdale Bay. The owners of Barisdale Estate run a bothy and bunkhouse for people to come and stay the night in, and open their field up to tent campers. After making my way off the boat, I noticed with a giggle that, while the other passengers who had chartered the vessel had loaded mountain bikes, tents and other paraphernalia to support a week-long adventure in the heart of this wild landscape, I carried all I needed on my back.

When I'd set out that morning, a thick, rainy mist had descended on the road, making me believe that today was going to be a typically wet Scottish day, often described by locals as 'dreich', a wonderfully pleasing word. I had layered up before I came, throwing on a long-sleeved woollen base layer and bracing myself for winter, but now the sun bore down on me intensely. I wandered along the pebble-encrusted beach, my feet crunching on the shells that were strewn along it before sinking with a satisfying plod into the sand. The mountains looked so perfect, so cinematically well proportioned and lit as though by spotlight, that it was hard to believe they were really there at all. I continued along the sand and then climbed up through the grass on a dirt road, where a sign pointed onwards for Barisdale. At this point the path seemed to split, with some of it backing off behind me, bound for Loch Hourn.

For those wanting to be even more puritanical than I was being walking in from Barrisdale Bay, there is another starting point for this landscape and that is at the head of Loch Hourn. Around 6 kilometres back from where I now stood, it begins not far from where the road in from civilisation ends, at a small farm where the owner runs a seasonal B&B. That sounds straightforward enough, but getting there is a really time-consuming exercise. Once you have left the main road, shortly after a turn-off near Fort Augustus, it's a 12-mile single-track road to the head of the loch. No matter how hard you try to go faster, it's an arduous and drawn-out drive that can take the best part of an hour and a half. It winds its way around dramatic drops and through scenery that's so good to look at, but you can't because you're way too busy trying to keep the car from careering off the road as locals (who are somehow driving cars that stick to the tarmac no matter what) head towards you at breakneck speed, leaving you to work out in a fluster just where the last passing place was.

Glad to have escaped such an ordeal, I began to walk at a steady and relaxed pace. There was just a single tent in the campsite, just one hardy soul who had decided that now was the right time of the year to sleep out in the open – and I admired them for that – but my pegs were set on a rather different place. As a keen wild camper, it might seem odd for me to end up staying on what is one of the few peninsulas in Scotland where the activity is actually discouraged, though not forbidden, in an attempt to keep man's interference with the wildlife to a minimum. I did, of course, have my tent with me and I was on the lookout for a suitable spot.

Passing the whitewashed buildings at Barisdale I continued on, practically panting in the heat of the ascent. I stopped halfway up the slope, at what must have been the only tree left on the hillside, and fought to catch my breath and regain my composure. Rolling up my sleeves, I walked over to the little stream and collected a handful of it in my cupped palms, then threw it over my head. I reached an instant clarity, my face tingling from the coldness thrown over its warm, reddened skin. It felt good.

Continuing on up, I passed a few other people all bound for Barisdale and a night in the bunkhouse. 'To the pub,' I answered simply as soon as anyone asked where I was off too, which was met by laughter and smiles. Soon I reached the saddle where the peaks of Stob a' Chearcaill and Luinne Bheinn scoop down to meet with a little shoulder of land, a place the Munro-baggers head to on their mission to tackle the mountains. From here I finally caught my first glimpse down into the valley that houses Loch an Dubh-Lochain, a big body of water that stretches on deceptively for about 2 kilometres then flows down a further 5 kilometres out to Loch Nevis at the end. In today's mild temperatures it glistened as though strewn with cut glass that caught the light with each breeze of the wind.

I sat up there for many minutes, and even walked out above the loch, toying with the idea of pitching a tent there, intrigued by the thought of waking up to such a view, stretching down not just across Knoydart but out over the open sea too. But the call of the coastline was too much for me to ignore and so I began my long descent into the valley. Sunny it may have been, but dry it was not, the recent weather having completely flooded the path in some places. I cut my way through it and listened with delight as the water sloshed at my feet.

Though long, it was one of the most peaceful stretches of water I had ever had the fortune to walk alongside. On the flanks of the hill to my right I watched as a herd of red deer paused to work out whether I was friend or foe before going back to munching at the grass. A huge stag with antlers like candelabras roamed above them, watching after his harem, looking majestic as he strutted his stuff.

In the air I could smell the grass as though it had been freshly cut – indeed, it felt and looked more like summer – and the colours of the plants belied their season. I swear that even from this distance I could pick up the aroma of the deer's fur, all wet and matted in a dew-like coating. Beside me, in between jumping from one patch of dry ground to another, I listened intently as the stream trickled and sputtered, gurgling the water as it flowed down the mountainside to fill the loch.

The smells, the sights, the sounds – they all felt so put together, like a Hollywood vision of a Scottish paradise – and I was completely taken in. A place of perfect peace. It seemed odd to think that, like so many of the most serene spots in the country, this one had a very sad history to it, one that was anything but peaceful.

In a tale that reads like a cinematic epic – probably one starring Russell Crowe and directed by James Cameron – Knoydart was the setting for a struggle between local crofters and rich landowners. In the mid nineteenth century, rather than relying on tourists to come and visit the novelty pub at Inverie, instead this peninsula was a place for working – for rearing cattle, farming the land and fishing in the water that surrounds it. However, Scotland was in the midst of its infamous Highland Clearances, a time when wealthy landowners decided that their plots could be used for a much more profitable purpose, such as sheep farming or the hosting of shooting parties (who would pay thousands to come and drink whisky, eat rich food and shoot wildlife). Knoydart was no different. The landowner decided she too wanted in on the profitable action and so schemed to rid herself of her crofters. She encouraged them to emigrate to Canada, and many did. Those who refused to leave were eventually forcibly evicted.

I looked up at the sky, which was filled with birds soaring overhead, enjoying the freedom of the thermals. The loch was rippling with the steady current of wind making its way across the surface. It would be hard to give up a life here in this wonderfully wild place, even if it was to start a new life somewhere overseas.

Continuing on the path I spotted a small white cross on the crest of a hillock below me. Many who see it incorrectly think it's a tribute to the 'Knoydart Seven', some locals, including some ex-soldiers just back from the Second World War in 1945, keen to carve a life out for themselves by working the land. When that was refused, they decided not to take no for an answer and set about farming several acres of the estate.

The landowners – Lord and Lady Brocket – were furious, and sought legal action to remove their squatters. What they didn't bank on was that the law was no longer in their favour. After the Second World War many locals around Britain were permitted to use land for their livelihood, which is what the crofters in Knoydart argued that they were doing in this instance. It seemed they would win, gaining support from MPs down in London and even managing to raise enough money from supporters to secure the services of a lawyer. Sadly, the solicitor advised them poorly, telling them they would have a better chance if they fought their case having got off the land. Lord and Lady Brocket seized the initiative and regained the land, whereupon support at Westminster for the would-be crofters fell away.

I pondered this as I reached the point immediately below the white cross, which is in fact a self-indulgent memorial erected by Lord Brocket himself to celebrate his family.

I didn't stop for too long here, instead following the path uphill into the much-needed cover of a few trees. I looked around me at some woodcarvings and took a pew on the bench that had been fashioned from one of the logs.

Those locals may have lost their land battles, but their actions did not go unnoticed, and their determination and courage were mimicked by the working-class generations that followed. They continued to challenge the Scottish landowners who were away for more time than they were around, and they ultimately established the rights that exist today. As of 1999, 71 square kilometres now make up the Knoydart Estate, which is owned by a foundation of locals and non-profit groups who work hard to protect the land from development and privatisation for the benefit of locals, walkers and wildlife alike. In a way, the Knoydart Seven did win, and it's not surprising that down at the local post office today there sits a simple memorial stone in their honour.

It was a happy thought and one that stuck in my head as I reached a gate that signposted the way down to the hamlet of Inverie. I followed the wide road where, as it met up with the tarmac track, a man bade me good evening.

'Have you booked your pub meal?' he asked.

'Oh, no – I think it will be OK?' It was more of a question than a reply.

'Hmm, not sure. I think it's actually quite expensive,' he added and I just smiled. For me, the location was simply priceless.

I decided to heed something of his advice, though, and so passed the converted church that is now a house and made a dash for The Old Forge.

Inside it's a fairly standard pub, apart from the fact that it sells a hell of a lot of memorabilia telling the world that you have visited the most remote pub on mainland Britain. For me, this was a wholly fitting place to reflect on my Extreme Sleeps Challenge.

The initial moment that sparked my love affair with wild camping and adventure generally was an argument with an Australian in a bar in Woolloomooloo, just outside Sydney. He had made me realise that, though I was well travelled, I knew shamefully little of my home country, and it was that conversation that saw me seeking out adventures closer to home. I raised my glass to him now, he who had set me off on this never-ending adventure of a lifetime, on my continual camping mission to find excitement in every facet of the UK – and I had found it in abundance.

Then I remembered the cyclist in Kendal, the one who had set me off on this more recent set of challenges. I smiled and raised a glass to him too, wondering if he would ever discover that he was the catalyst for a whole raft of adventures to have the word 'extreme' steadfastly associated with them.

I ate the food hungrily at The Old Forge. The songs of ceilidh rung across the beam-vaulted ceilings and idle chatter about the unexpected bout of sunshine sung from everyone's lips. The unmistakable scent of spilled beer was welcoming in the air, and the clank and scrape of people happily eating provided an extra layer to this friendly gathering.

When I was done I made my way back alongside the road, where the last of the ferries were taking off. In the shorter daylight hours at this time of year, this place, which can become so busy in the high summer, all at once becomes almost eerily quiet. I took a moment to just stand and be absorbed by it, by the silence, away from the crowds.

I passed behind the bunkhouses – I had decided to camp on Long Beach, the one and only officially designated camping spot in Inverie. With many places to pitch at my disposal, I opted for a spot as close to the water as I could get without pitching on the sand itself.

A few flies buzzed about me lazily, not really seeming sure that they should be there. I wedged the tent pegs into the loose soil and waited at my tent door for the inevitable sunset. Soon I got what I wanted, the sky turning almost crimson in the evening light as the giant orb set in the sky, casting shadows not just on where I sat with my tent, but on the whole landscape behind me too.

As the water went mirror-like against the horizon, I too found myself getting a little reflective. I never thought when I was drinking in Kendal that I would, by chance, strike up a conversation with someone who would set in motion a plan that would lead me to become the first woman to sleep at the extremes of Britain.

It's funny how one journey can lead to another, more unexpected destination. I couldn't have realised that a revisit to Fisherfield – somewhere that I had been to several times – would enable me to discover a little innocuous patch of land that I had never bothered to pay heed to before. I had never considered that a stay on the summit of my local highest peak – on a day when I had merely been trying to escape a particularly bad bout of TV – would see me become the first woman to sleep on the highest peaks in Wales, England and Scotland. And I never saw it coming that, once I had achieved these particular goals, I would merely shrug them off with the realisation that, while challenges are all well and good, they are just the vehicles, the means, to force you to try out other destinations that had so far remained off radar.

Doing my 3 Peaks Sleeps on Snowdon, Scafell Pike and Ben Nevis had proven to me that I could deal with any kind of weather the UK could throw at me, but had also shown me that sometimes – just sometimes – in the hills, man-made structures can be of use, even where, little by little, nature has started to reclaim them.

My night on Corrachadh Mòr had taken me to a part of Scotland that I otherwise would never have bothered visiting – so inaccessible is it compared to other good mountainous destinations nearby. I had made myself a promise to revisit it for more wild camps at another time.

Visiting Dunnet Head for a night atop the cliffs had proved to me just how important these far-flung points of the compass were during our major world wars, and had also shown me the value of neglecting the headline-stealing locations to seek out the lesser-known and, more often than not, crowd-free options that usually lurk nearby.

Plodding my way through bogland in a misty damp night to reach the much-disputed centremost point of mainland Britain had been a true celebration of the work of the campaigners who had opened up the once-shut-down Forest of Bowland for walkers like me. Despite the weather, and the signs claiming that everything up there was either private or forbidden, I had proven to myself that there are still corners of our country where you can truly be alone and get away from it all, and that ignoring signs often brings with it the most fun you can have in the outdoors.

My foray east for perhaps the most urban and unglamorous sleep of my camping career had, surprisingly, rather than leaving me sad about the future of this landmark, left me with a real sense of hope for a bright future for the place.

Driving from Lowestoft to Holme had taught me that doing my Extreme Sleeps Challenge had become as much about the moments in between the sleeps as it was about the sleeps themselves. The stolen cheery conversations with staff at services, whose whole life is dedicated to one-off chats with strangers moving somewhere else, with very few repeat dialogues – at least not with the same people – are fused within the memories of the wild places I visited.

Unlike the other sleeps, a night in the woods at Holme Fen showed that man's determination to control the wild can sometimes damage it in more ways than we know, and that sometimes allowing it to do what it wants to do naturally, unfettered by us, would be the most positive course of action we could afford it.

Making myself go back to properly sleep on The Ben was a great moment for me, a time when I took responsibility to see a challenge through from start to finish even when I didn't really want to.

Going back to sleep on the Lizard, as I first had several years previously when I began undertaking my 'extreme sleeps', reminded me just how far I have come as a wild camper, worrying less about people happening upon me while I sleep and no longer fearing ghosts when walking in the dark.

Sleeping in a bivvy for many of the sleeps on this challenge saw me admiring the landscape from a different perspective, albeit a slightly damper one. Without the more sturdy structures of tent walls giving me the space to move around and sit up, I somehow felt one step closer to the environment, as if for a short while I had merged with it, become a part of it, been camouflaged by it.

By far the most unexpected part of my whole adventure had been my first night on Ben Nevis, when I had thought for a minute that I would have to call the whole Extreme Sleeps Challenge off. But, deciding that beautifying that wild place by carrying down two bags of discarded rubbish that wasn't even my own would be more of an achievement than any sleep challenge could possibly offer, was a moment when I realised the kind of person I had become. One who would put caring for nature over and above conquering it, someone who would rather unite with it in a sort of partnership than become the master of it, and that was definitely the sort of camper I wanted to be.

As I sat on Long Beach on Knoydart, reflecting on where I'd come from and where I'd been, I wondered whether, if I had gone and spoken to the person I used to be before I'd taken the river crossing at Glencoul, and told myself that, while I would suffer momentarily, becoming stuck in the fast-flowing water and having to pull myself out fighting off hypothermia, I would rise from the icy water with a fresh perspective, a kind of natural rebirth – would I still have attempted to cross it?

The irony of my current location was not lost on me. That I, an ardent wild camper, one who had started off nearly dying to get to a patch of wilderness, and after one chance conversation had flung myself to the four corners of the mainland to seek out the ultimate pitch, sleeping on the highest, centremost and lowest points of the country along the way, had found the perfect camp spot right here on a paid-for campsite.

I looked about me at the fading light, the mountains across the water becoming faint lines on a grey canvas, the grass swaying in the breeze, the lights in the bundle of buildings at Inverie switching off, and a whole gamut of stars spreading themselves above me like a dazzling duvet cover. It had taken a far less extreme challenge to find my perfect paradise, my moment of perfection amid all others, but here it was – for the small price of just £4.

People sometimes ask me why I wild camp. What's the point? Where has it taken you? And I tell them that it takes me anywhere I want to go, because having all I need on my back, being totally self-sufficient, means that my journey is limitless.

For me wild camping is neither a start nor an end. It's not a noun, a simple descriptor or even a verb, a doing word, it is merely a conjunction – the and-and-and that connects many destinations and multiple goals, and leads to myriad adventures. And if you look at it that way when, like me, you complete a set series of events like the Extreme Sleeps Challenge and ask yourself where you should go now that your goal has been achieved, the answer is simple – it really doesn't matter as long as you keep going. The real answer for me is that my own adventure, my personal one that began many years ago when I first headed off into the hinterland of Snowdonia National Park on my own in a quest to fall in love again with the country I call home, continues to keep me going. Regardless of what I thought I was doing when, or where I believed I was going, I have been on the same path the whole time, continuing to push myself as an adventurer, to experience as many wild places as I can, and to prove to myself that I can be self-sufficient. And that journey, that mammoth adventure I never even realised I had set off on, will never truly end. So, although the challenges I set this time round were finished, nothing else is.

It's a funny place to be, realising that after all these years of striving to find adventure, I had been living it all along. Here on Knoydart I sat, having finished another grand tour of Great Britain, from its highest points to its lowest, through service stations and B roads and single-track gravel paths and motorways, often taking full days to reach my next destination, to hide out and wait for night to fall before I pitched up. I was utterly contented, and, as I zipped up my tent for the evening, closing a fabric door on this crazy quest, I felt my brain already working on plans for where I might go next.

You may well be confused with me ending my story here, asking yourself: is this a beginning or an end? But I'm going to leave it for you to decide. For here in these pages I am simply sharing my experiences to hopefully ignite a similar light inside you. May the closing of this book lead you to a tent-bound quest for adventure, where the landscapes are captivating, the experiences life-changing, and the possibilities endless.

EXTREME SLEEPS
Adventures of a Wild Camper

Phoebe Smith

£8.99

Paperback

ISBN: 978-1-84953-393-5

I had become officially infatuated with what I called 'extreme sleeping' – a kind of addictive high-adrenaline sport – but rather than being defined by pushing the boundaries of physical activity, my particular pursuit was marked by a distinct lack of it.

Veteran globetrotter Phoebe Smith sets out to prove that outdoor adventures are available in the UK which rival anything found elsewhere in the world. In this sometimes scary, frequently funny and intriguing journey around the country, Phoebe attempts to discover and conquer its wildest places.

From spending the night in the decaying wreckage of a World War Two bomber at Bleaklow to pitching next to the adrenaline-inducing sheer drops of Lizard Point, Phoebe's extreme sleeps defy her perceptions of the great outdoors and teach her about herself along the way.

MUD, SWEAT & GEARS

Cycling From Land's End to John O'Groats (Via the Pub)

Ellie Bennett

£8.99

Paperback

ISBN: 978-1-84953-220-4

As Ellie's fiftieth birthday approaches and her ambitions of a steady income, a successful career and an ascent of Everest seem as far away as ever, she begins to doubt she's capable of achieving anything at all. So when her best friend Mick suggests a gruelling cycle ride from Land's End to John o'Groats, she takes up the challenge.

They opt for the scenic route which takes them along cycle paths, towpaths and the back roads and byways of Britain, unable to resist sampling local beers in the pubs they pass along the way. But as the pints start to stack up faster than the miles they're putting under their tyres, Ellie wonders if they'll ever make it to the finishing line...

Have you enjoyed this book?
If so, why not write a review on your favourite website?

If you're interested in finding out more about our books,
find us on Facebook at **Summersdale Publishers** and follow us
on Twitter at **@Summersdale**.

Thanks very much for buying this Summersdale book.

www.summersdale.com